"Recipes Are Like Pearls … lovely, but not useful until strung together"

A Chanticleer Inn B&B
Breakfast Cookbook

by Ellen C. Campbell

CHANTICLEER
INN

Recipes, text and food photography by Ellen Campbell,
Ashland Chanticleer Inn LLC,
120 Gresham St. Ashland OR, 97520
www.ashlandbnb.com

Cover design and layout by Chris Molé,
Chris Molé Designs
40 Water St., Ashland OR, 97520

Cover photo of Ellen taken by David Bjurstrom
David Bjurstrom Studio and Gallery
64 N. Pioneer St., Ashland OR, 97520

Publication layout by Diana Donaldson
http://www.didoart.net

ISBN: 978-0-9799111-0-1

Address editorial sales rights and permission inquiries to Ellen Campbell at 120 Gresham St. Ashland OR, 97520.

In memory of Connie Pious

This book would never have been started without her loving encouragement.

Acknowledgments

Most creative projects involve more than just one person: this book is no exception. First my gratitude must go to my staff at the Chanticleer, Laurie Myrick, Audrey Copeland, Daviana Jacquat, Michiko Wisdom, Jamie Queensbury-Gunson, Mary Hall, Niki Jacquat, and Jennifer Conshue. Over the years, they have provided helpful, honest feedback, and suggestions that have improved or refined many of these recipes.

Thanks goes to David Bjurstrom for taking the cover picture of me and to his partner William Bloodgood for so ably assisting and setting up the "photo shoot."

Leanne Ulvang kindly provided editorial review and feedback. To Diana Donaldson for helping me in the final publication layout before going to press.

During a 2003 visit, Carli Scott a friend and frequent guest, created interesting and appealing names for each dish she consumed during her stay. Throughout this book, many of the recipes have Carli's imaginative monikers. If the name is boring, let the reader know that Carli has yet to name that dish.

Table of Contents

Introduction

This cookbook got its start because so many guests request recipes. What better compliment can a cook receive, apart perhaps from plates coming back into the kitchen swiped clean or requests for second helpings? So this book is for all our guests and friends who wish to replicate the Chanticleer Inn breakfasts at home.

More than a compilation of recipes, this book is designed and structured to assist cooks to prepare a complete breakfast feast. How many times have you found an intriguing potentially delicious recipe? You ponder its possibilities. You imagine how it will taste; then the inevitable question pops up: So what do I serve with it? Absent any suggestions, too many times that recipe is never prepared; it remains on the page, just a possibility. Any significant culinary experience involves more than one recipe - usually 3 to 4 working in concert. Thus the title of this book, "Recipes Are Like Pearls...lovely but not useful until strung together."

Another feature of this cookbook is a separate index for special dietary requirements. No more flipping through an entire cookbook, repetitively reading lists of ingredients to find a recipe that might suit.

These dishes have been developed and served from a true home kitchen. Many of our recipes have evolved over a few years, each developed and improved upon by feedback from the inn's staff and guests.

To better ensure repeatability, all appliances and utensils called for in this book are what most home cooks already have in their kitchens. The preparation instructions call for as few utensils, bowls and other gadgets as possible, thus streamlining the preparation, and reducing cooking and cleaning time.

Breakfast ingredients and sources:
When available in the markets, I buy locally grown fresh fruits and vegetables. As much as possible, I support the local growers, many of whom are organic. We are very lucky in southern Oregon.

This region provides wonderful world-renown produce. My next preference is fruits and vegetables that come from California and Washington.

Talk about locally grown ... over the years, as I've developed the garden Chanticleer breakfasts increasingly include organic herbs, flowers, fruits, and vegetables from our backyard. I will expand that trend for as long as the gates and netting succeed in keeping out the deer. The Chanticleer garden is also blessed with two prolific fig trees. In mid-summer we get a small bonus crop, called a breba, and then in the fall a much larger and longer-lasting crop of luscious figs. This explains why there are a few fig recipes in this cookbook.

Breakfast Room*,*
image by William Wisdom

Chanticleer Inn Breakfasts

Over the last six years, we've come to understand that a complete breakfast is the most luxurious meal of the day. Except on vacations or during special holidays, there is no time nowadays to savor and to linger over breakfasts with friends and family. That's why we feel it important to offer a full gourmet breakfast for our guests.

For us the ingredients for a Chanticleer Morning are engaging guests, sociable hosts, and strong fresh organic coffee, followed by a creative 2-course breakfast.

Chanticleer Inn's Breakfast, As Our Guests Tell It ...

Some of our regular and longstanding guests wrote testimonials for the cookbook. Expecting short blurbs of one or two pithy sentences, I was surprised and very pleased by the veritable essays written by my kind guests. Perhaps for some, writing about food gets the creative juices, as well as the digestive juices, flowing.

So rather than me telling you about Chanticleer Inn's breakfast, I've decided that my guests do a far better job than I ...

Leanne Ulvang, Chico, CA
"We who have stayed at the Chanticleer Inn have been awaiting this cookbook with tongues at the ready. Ellen concocts menus of foods that complement each other, using in-season fruits and flowers. The flavors meld deliciously and at the end of the meal, we leave replete, looking forward to the next sumptuous breakfast. Now we have the opportunity to create some of these feasts for our friends and families!"

Barry and Irene Grenier, and Mitzi and Bob Konevich, Los Altos California

"Ellen carefully and creatively blends the fruits of her garden and the creations of her kitchen into a beautiful and fragrant palate of morning treats -- often a fresh fig from the tree just outside the door, and always the edible petals of freshly harvested flowers.

As we dreamily awaken in the lovely abode known as Chanticleer Inn, we are greeted with the smells of fresh coffee and a baked confection which we might not be able to identify but which we anticipate to be healthy, perhaps fruity, and always, always scrumptious. We are never disappointed when we arrive at table ... there awaiting each guest is a personal table setting with a lovely array of fruit and perhaps yogurt, a proper amount of protein – sometimes chicken sausage, turkey bacon or cheese, and then the main dish ... lively with flavor and always a recipe that only a person with panache and mirth would create ... dishes with an Asian hint, a Mexican flare, a French or Italian aura, French toast to melt in the mouth, fluffy omelets to rave about, the puffy muffin whose fragrance lured guests from the warmth of bed, real maple syrup or homemade pastries ... the ultimate comfort foods! Above all, the sincere interest of Ellen and Howie in the histories of every guest and our day-to-day doings, their hospitality and their big hearts infuse the atmosphere and make our meals taste all the more lovely. Our hosts keep the cookie jar thoughtfully replenished with treats ... sometimes chocolate, sometimes fruit laden and always the right balance of sweet and savory; that way no one tell who has sneaked a snack or two at bedtime!"

Larry and Leah Westmoreland, Edmond, Oklahoma

"The important thing to know about breakfast at the Chanticleer is that it is so much more than breakfast. Of course, there is the wonderful food, but before that, the mix of aromas drifting up to "Aerie," the pre-breakfast coffee and conversation.

Then, the attractively arranged fresh fruit and edible flowers, the unhurried ambiance, the always smiling staff, the animated discussion of the previous night's plays, the making of plans for the

day's adventures, and the presence of Ellen and Howie making the orchestration of a beautiful breakfast look easy."

Jane and Lou Carlos, San Leandro, CA
"I always look forward to breakfast, usually early. The current newspapers are there to check the headlines, baseball scores, and weather. And the decaf is waiting for me (and sometimes others) indicated with a gauzy ribbon tied to the handle with a gold coffee pot charm. The decaf warms me and wakes me up with its 2% caffeine!

There may be other guests there as well. Some ready to chat about last night's plays or just as interested as I am in the New York Times, Wall Street Journal, or Oregonian, and coffee, and all is quiet. Lou is one of the quiet ones as well as me.

Then presently breakfast is served at tables for six or four. The first course is fruit, one of my favorites. Ellen says she never knows what the breakfast will be until she shops the day before. She has a knack for always choosing the best in freshness, taste, and appearance, and sometimes we're treated to fresh figs from her garden. The garnish is usually an edible flower, which I can never eat, enjoying it with my eyes instead.

Ellen alternates between sweet and savory dishes for the entree. I love them both. Favorites with my husband are the buttermilk coffee cake and the waffles. She made the waffles when she asked Lou what he liked best at breakfast, and she came through. Not an easy dish to fix simultaneously for five or six others (for meat least), but she brought it off handily. For me the chicken sausages are a favorite, too. They're always cooked just right, tender and juicy. I've tried them at home and they don't come out the same. Some dishes were new to me, like the Dutch Babies. Delicious. And the story Ellen told about an incident with this dish was so amusing.

Ellen looks out for the health of her guests. Of course, asking them about their diet restrictions and insuring them she can work around it; but at the same time preparing such items as chicken sausages, instead of their fat-laden cousins.

The conversation around the table will be about the plays, the food, where guests are from and where they've traveled. And Howie is always there to add to the conversation, or start a new topic that usually is of interest to one or more of us. Ellen joins us when she can; and I especially enjoy it when we can linger over coffee, maybe just a few of us, and talk and talk and talk."

Timothy Hill, Bend, OR
"The food was exceptional. The breakfast was comprised of two courses. The fruit course seemed like you were walking into an orchard as you were presented with a perfectly ripe half-pear garnished with yogurt, orange slices and berries. Following the fruit was the hot food course, which consisted of baked French toast that was hot and melted in your mouth with a hint of cinnamon. It also was garnished with sliced fruit. It reminded me of hot bread pudding with subtle spicing and flavors. Each course was like a composed picture. You hated to disturb it but it demanded to be eaten with relish. I cannot say enough nice things about the Ashland Chanticleer Inn, a truly superb place to stay."

Valerie and Bob Winsor, Seattle, WA
"Ellen creates knockout breakfasts at the Chanticleer. Guests awaken to aromas wafting from the kitchen and are rewarded with well-balanced meals featuring tasty fruit concoctions, hearty protein creations, and tempting, yet not too sweet, carbohydrate delicacies.

My favorites include the "melt in your mouth" Almond Pear Clafouti, Mango Berry Mousse, Rustic Russet Pie and Ellen's own Turkey Sausage.

If you are fortunate enough to stay for three or four days you sample a different menu every day. Ellen has many tricks up her sleeve and is a wizard with fresh fruits and vegetables. The Yam-crusted Frittata is not to be missed!!"

Leonard and Beth Soloway, Lafayette, CA
"One of the many attributes that make the Chanticleer a great bed and breakfast is the breakfast. They are varied and delectable. Sweet, savory or simple, all dishes are well prepared, very

often original in concept and always have excellent taste. Ellen Campbell definitely knows how to cook."

Jack and Joan Leversee, Seattle WA
"What is the ideal way to start your day, on vacation or not? Prepare some of the wonderful recipes from Ellen Campbell's cookbook.

You will find the dishes delicious, healthy, appealing to the eyes and the palate. And one does not need to be a Master Chef to prepare the items in this book. Try 'em; you'll love 'em."

Laurel Przybylski, Oakland, CA
"Breakfasts with Ellen at the Chanticleer are adventures. The food is a treat for the eyes, nose, and taste buds.   We always enjoy the thoughtfully prepared food and pleasant conversation with our hosts and fellow guests. We come back year after year, knowing it will always be the same...Warm, welcoming, wonderful"

The Chanticleer Inn

The Chanticleer Inn, a 1920 renovated Craftsman, is the oldest continuing B&B in Ashland offering welcoming hospitality, comfortable elegance, expansive secluded gardens, and views of the Cascade mountains across the valley. Located in a quiet historic neighborhood, the Chanticleer is a short stroll to the Oregon Shakespeare Festival and downtown Ashland. We celebrated its 25th anniversary with the 2006 season.

If our guests are not attending plays, walking about town, or taking one of the numerous day trips, they may be found relaxing in the garden with a fish pond, snoozing in the hammock watching the world go by from the porch swing, or curling up by a fire with port and a good book.

The Chanticleer Inn from the side yard
photo by David Cooper

Ashland: Where Nature Meets the Arts

For many the "Ashland Experience" is three-fold: come for first-rate theater, stay at a lovely B&B, and dine at fabulous restaurants. However, there is much more to Ashland and the Rogue Valley.

Charm of Ashland is found in its wealth of theatres, art galleries, parks, shops, museums, day spas and historic neighborhoods - - all nestled at the base of the Siskiyou Mountains and all within walking distance of the Chanticleer. If you have a willingness to jump in your car for some short day trips, you can expand your experience by visiting such area attractions as Crater Lake, Jacksonville, the Britt Music Festival, the Rogue Valley's many wineries, antique shops, and Harry & David's headquarters.

Ashland is a performing arts town! There are at least five "Off Bardway" theaters, as the locals fondly refer to the wonderful innovative and avant-garde theater companies in and around Ashland. Most of these venues are within walking distance of the Chanticleer Inn and many of them run during the winter months. For more details please see our website in the Area Attractions section.

And what about our guests who love the outdoors and want more adventure? The Rogue Valley is a veritable wonderland of great terrain and natural resources for rafting, kayaking, fishing, skiing, hiking, snowshoeing, biking, etc. Again we can direct our guests to local adventure outfitters and lots of ideas for things to do through our website.

No matter how hard you try, it's almost impossible to describe Southern Oregon's breathtaking beauty. While exploring the Siskiyou and Cascade mountain ranges you can discover the rarity of flora and fauna for which they're famous. And lovers of birds, butterflies, and wildflowers will come to understand why the World Wildlife Foundation calls this area the "Galapagos of North America."

Menus and Special Diets or ... "stringing it all together"

Much more than a compilation of recipes, this book is organized so it is easy to "string together" recipes to create sumptuous breakfasts feasts or brunches for family and friends.

At the Chanticleer, we do not repeat a recipe during a guest's stay and each day we alternate between sweet and savory main dishes. The average stay is 2-3 days, but it's not unusual to have guests who stay longer. This means we need enough recipes to create a series of unique menus for quite a few days. Furthermore, we also consider the number of guests, seasonal availability of fruit and vegetables, and the occasional guest with dietary restrictions and allergies.

Given these constraints and policies, as a novice innkeeper I found creating menus the most challenging part of planning breakfasts. Menu planning finally got a little easier when I settled on a general format: three to four prepared items served in two courses. The first course focuses on fruit and pastry; the second course features one substantial dish and a side of meat or potatoes.

If a first course dish combines both fruit and pastry, such as our fruit crumble, then we serve a 3-item breakfast. The crumble is quite hearty and with a large serving, guests do not miss a side of pastry. Or if the main dish consists primarily of bread, such as the baked French toast, we will also serve a 3-item breakfast.

This cookbook is organized based on our menu format. The rough and ready heuristic for creating a breakfast menu is this:

1. Select one recipe from the Pastries chapter and another recipe from the First Courses chapter.

2. Decide on a sweet or savory breakfast and select one recipe from either the Sweet or Savory main courses chapter, making sure the main ingredients and the spices and/or herbs of the recipes you have chosen are not repetitive.

3. Select to serve a side of potatoes or breakfast meat, such as turkey bacon or chicken sausage.

Dietary Concerns

Many of our guests are health conscious and some have serious dietary requirements. Even though guests are here for a short time and are on holiday, I still feel the need to respect and support my guests' special dietary requirements, choices, and preferences. Sometimes, my guests want "to cheat," and we try our best to assist in that too. Many guests appreciate dishes lower in fat, so they don't have to be so vigilant at dinner in many of Ashland's fine restaurants.

Also one of the unusual features of this cookbook is a separate index for special dietary requirements. In this way, readers/cooks may easily find recipes that comply with specific restrictions or requirements, such as, lactose or gluten intolerance, vegan, etc. No more flipping through an entire cookbook, repetitively reading lists of ingredients to find a recipe that might suit.

In 2002, our first season, I stopped adding salt to all recipes and made salt and pepper shakers available for those who want to add more seasoning. I proceeded in the next two seasons to develop low-fat and non-fat dishes to the recipe repertoire and to change existing recipes to become more low fat. Many of the recipes in this book provide alternative ingredients so a cook may adjust the amount or type of fat. For period of time in the 2005 season, I eliminated processed sugar from my personal diet, as a consequence some of the recipes now indicate sugar alternatives or are completely free of sugar.

First Courses

Regardless of the title "First Courses" most of these dishes can be tasty and healthy "last courses." Originally, some of these recipes started as desserts. With less sugar, more fruit, different spices, and a wave of the hand they were transformed into breakfast starters.

For a second course pairing all of these recipes may easily be served with any of the savory dishes. With a sweet second course, some the first course recipes will go better than others. One needs to be sure not to repeat the same fruits or base sauce when pairing these first courses with a sweet main dish.

Caramelized Fruit with Ricotta & Cream Cheese

6 servings
Preheat broiler
Use a cookie sheet with edges
Use 6 dessert bowls

Note: Consider using six large fresh plums. Broiling releases a red-purple juice that contrasts beautifully with the cheese or yogurt base.

Ingredients

- 1/2 cup or 4 oz non-fat ricotta
- 1/2 cup or 4 oz Neufchâtel cream cheese
- 2-4 tablespoons honey (to taste) or Splenda
- 1 teaspoon vanilla extract
- 1/2 teaspoon almond extract
- 6 fresh apricots, plums, or 12 figs, cut off stems and halved lengthwise
- Brown sugar
- Garnish: mint sprigs

Directions

In a medium bowl with a hand mixer, blend the cheeses; add honey and extracts. Evenly divide the cheese mixture among small dessert bowls.

Place fruit cut side up on a cookie sheet and place approximately 1/2 to 1 teaspoon of brown sugar on each fruit. Broil fruit until brown sugar is bubbling.

Place 2-4 fruit halves in each bowl and spoon any melted brown sugar on top of the cheese mixture. Garnish with mint sprigs

Optional, spoon 1-2 tablespoons of a fruit sauce over the fruit

For a non-fat version of this recipe, replace the ricotta-cream cheese mixture with yogurt sauces.

Figs with a Raspberry Coulis

4 servings
Preheat broiler
Use flameproof baking dish or cookie sheet with edges

Ingredients

- 1 (10-oz) package frozen or fresh raspberries in syrup, thawed
- 8 fresh figs, trimmed and halved lengthwise
- 1/2 tablespoon brown sugar for each fig
- 1/2 cup non-fat vanilla yogurt or 1/2 cup of non-fat plain yogurt with a teaspoon of vanilla essence (for a vegan alternative: soy yogurt)

Directions

Force raspberries through a fine sieve into a bowl to remove seeds. Set bowl aside.

Sprinkle cut side of figs with brown sugar and place, sugared sides up, in a flameproof baking dish or cookie sheet with edges. Broil about 4 inches from heat until tops are bubbling and lightly browned, approximately 2 to 4 minutes.

Spoon 1-1/2 tablespoons raspberry coulis onto each of 4 dessert plates. Spoon a heaping tablespoon of yogurt in center of each, then arrange 4 fig halves on top of yogurt.

Figs in Red-Wine Syrup

4 servings
Use kitchen string; a 4-inch square of cheesecloth

Note: This dish also goes well with Stilton cheese or smoked
meats.

Ingredients

- 2 (3 by 1/2-inch) fresh lemon peel strips (without the pith)
- 1 (1 1/2 inch) cinnamon stick
- 6 black peppercorns
- 1 1/2 cups dry red wine
- 1/2 cup water
- 1/4 cup sugar
- 1 cup dried figs (1/2 lb; preferably Calimyrna), trimmed and
  each fig cut lengthwise into 3 slices
- 3 tablespoons fresh lemon juice
- 1/2 - 3/4 cup plain low-fat or non-fat yogurt (optionally, plain
  soy yogurt)

Directions

Tie lemon peel strips, cinnamon, and peppercorns together in a
cheesecloth bag.

Bring wine, water, sugar, and cheesecloth bag to a boil in a 1-
1/2quart heavy saucepan, stirring until sugar is dissolved. Boil
syrup until reduced to about 1-1/2 cups, 8 to 10 minutes

Add figs and simmer, covered, until soft and plump, 25 to 30
minutes.

Discard cheesecloth bag and stir lemon juice into fig mixture.

Cool at least 1 hour. Serve warm or at room temperature, topped
with yogurt or crème fraiche.

Fruit Crumble

6-8 servings
Preheat oven to 400°F
Use 8x8 baking dish and a food processor with an S-blade
Recipe easily doubles, for 12 servings use a 13x9 baking dish

Note: For a gluten-free version, exclude the flour, and increase
the nuts and oatmeal.

Ingredients

- Fruit, cut in wedges or large chunks, enough to fill the baking
dish 2/3 up the side. Use one or more of: apples, apricots,
berries, cherries, nectarines, peaches, pears, pineapple, plums
and/or strawberries."
- 2 tablespoons orange juice
- teaspoons each cinnamon and allspice.
- 3/4 cup whole wheat flour (optional: all-purpose flour)
- 1/2 cup brown sugar (optional: Splenda may be substituted)
- 3/4 cup + 1/4 cup almonds, whole
- 1/4 cup oatmeal
- 1 stick (1/2 cup) unsalted or sweet butter, cut into chunks. (Low-
fat and nondairy option: part Full Spectrum Spread and part
vegetable oil)
- Optional: 1/8-1/4 cup grated or shredded coconut

Directions

Evenly spread the cut fruit in a baking dish. Drizzle 2 tablespoons
of orange juice over fruit and sprinkle with spices.

If mixing fruit that cooks at different rates, then microwave the
fruit (e.g., apples and pears) that takes longer to cook for 3-5
minutes before adding the softer fruit.

Pulse flour, sugar, and 3/4 cup almonds in a food processor until
nuts are well chopped. Add butter and pulse until mixture begins
to clump, then add the remaining 1/4 cup almonds, oatmeal and
optionally the coconut, briefly pulse to coarsely chop almonds.

Spread crumble topping over fruit. Bake crumble in middle of the oven until fruit is tender and topping is golden brown, 25 to 30 minutes.

Honey-Cream Cheese Stuffed Peaches

Serves 4-6
Small dessert bowls per person
Hand-held mixer or small food processor

Ingredients

- One medium or large ripe peach per person
- One 8-oz package of cream cheese; may be "lite" or whole (Optional: Neufchatel cheese - texture and taste is similar to cream cheese, but it is lower in fat)
- Honey, to taste
- Vanilla (1/2 - 1 teaspoon)
- Optional: 1/2 - 1 teaspoon almond extract

Directions

At the stem end, cut the top off (about 1/2 inch), with tongs pull out the pit. You'll have to wiggle and twist a little bit to extract the pit. If the edges are untidy don't worry the cream cheese will cover it.

At the other end of the peach, take a tiny slice off the bottom, so that the peach will be able to "sit up" on the dish. Place each peach in a dessert bowl.

In a mixing bowl with a hand mixer, blend the cream cheese, honey, vanilla, and optionally extract to taste. The mixture should be a consistency that can be piped.

Pipe the cream cheese mixture into each peach cavity. With any remaining cream cheese mixture decoratively pipe around serving dishes.

Drizzle warmed honey over peach. Garnish with flowers or mint

Mango Berry Mousse

Serves 6-8
Prepare 4 hours before serving or the night before
Use 6-8 six-ounce ramekins or custard cups
Use a food processor with an S-blade

Ingredients

- 2 packets of unflavored gelatin
- 2 cups fresh mango, peeled and pitted
- 1 large ripe banana
- Sugar to taste
- 1/2 teaspoon vanilla extract
- Optional 1/2 teaspoon ground ginger
- 2 cups non-fat plain yogurt (alternatively, soy yogurt)
- 1/2 pint of blueberries or blackberries enough to line the bottom of each ramekin
- 18-24 orange slices, cut in half rounds – 3 half rounds per ramekin
- 6-8 sprigs of mint

Directions

Sprinkle gelatin over 1/4 cup cold water, then stir to allow the gelatin to bloom.

Divide the berries among the ramekins (see note below). Place three orange slices against the sides of each ramekin.

In a food processor, purée the mango and banana; then add the vanilla and the sugar to taste.

Liquefy the gelatin in a microwave, 15-30 seconds on high. Add the yogurt and gelatin to the fruit purée; process until well blended.

Pour the mousse in all the ramekins. Chill in refrigerator until well set, overnight or at least 4 hours.

To serve, turn each mousse out onto a small plate or a dessert bowl. Garnish with a sprig of mint

Note: As the ramekin functions as a mould, lots of fruity additions can be used to dazzling effect. Select colors that compliment or contrast with the predominant orange of the mousse, such as, banana slices, strawberries, blueberries, blackberries, and/or kiwi slices.

Oranges in Cardamom Syrup

Serves 6
May be made the night before

Ingredients

- 2 five-inch long strips of orange peel
- 10 medium-sized navel oranges
- 1 teaspoon ground cardamom
- 6 cups water
- 3 cups sugar
- 2 five-inch long strips of lemon peel
- 2 cinnamon sticks

Directions

With a vegetable peeler, remove 2 five-inch strips of peel from a navel orange and a lemon: reserve the 4 strips.

Cut of the rind including the white piths from the oranges. Cut the oranges lengthwise in half, then crosswise into 1/3-inch-thick slices; place slices in a bowl.

Mix water, sugar, lemon and orange peels, cardamom, and cinnamon sticks in a pan; bring to boil.

Reduce heat to low; simmer until mixture is reduced to 1 1/2 cup, about 50 minutes. Cool syrup for 10 minutes.

Pour the warm syrup over oranges through a sieve, and chill at least 6 hours or overnight. Discard solids in the sieve.

Serve oranges in syrup in small dessert bowls or as a topping over yogurt or ice cream.

Pear Boat

Serves 6
Six dessert bowls

Note: Prepare the yogurt cream about 8 hours before use.

Ingredients

- 1/2-3/4 cup non- or low-fat plain yogurt (or soy yogurt)
- Sugar, to taste
- 3 large very ripe, very juicy pears
- Colorful fruit, such as:
- 1/2 cup blueberries or blackberries
- Kiwi, slices
- Strawberries, sliced
- Grapes, halved
- Garnish with mint sprigs

Directions

Drain yogurt in a paper towel-lined sieve set into a bowl in refrigerator for about 8 hours. Before serving, transfer yogurt cream to a clean bowl and stir in sugar to sweeten, but not to remove the tartness.

Slice the pears lengthwise, and on the base side (uncut side) of the pear, take a tiny slice off the bottom, so that the pear will be stable in the serving dish. Using paring knife cut away the stem and using a small melon-baller or a metal teaspoon scoop out the pear core.

Mound the yogurt cream in the center of each pear. Decoratively place the sliced fruit on top of the yogurt cream and garnish with mint sprigs.

Plums in Orange Sauce

Serves 6
Six dessert bowls

Ingredients

- 1/4 cup unsalted or sweet butter (see note)
- Zest and juice of 2 oranges, about 1/2 cup
- 3 tablespoons brown sugar
- 1 tablespoon cinnamon
- 2 teaspoons vanilla extract
- 8-10 plums, pitted and sliced in bite-sized wedges - may also use peaches or nectarines
- Approximately, 1 1/4 cup non-fat yogurt (alternatively, soy yogurt or, for a richer base use ricotta-cream cheese)
- Garnish: mint sprigs

Directions

In medium saucepan, melt butter over medium-low heat.

Stir in all ingredients, except plums and yogurt, and simmer gently to infuse flavors.

Turn off heat, add plums and gently toss.

Divide yogurt among 6 dessert bowls and then place plums atop yogurt. Drizzle remaining plum/orange sauce over plums. Garnish with mint sprigs.

Note: For a non-fat version, omit the butter completely. For low fat or vegan version, use a butter substitute, such as Full Spectrum.

Poached Pears

Serves 8
8 dessert bowls

Note: This recipe is best made at least 30 minutes in advance to give the pears time to cool.

Ingredients

- 4 medium/large pears, Bosc, Anjou, or Bartlett
- 1 cup orange juice
- Water, enough to just cover the pears

Directions

Halve, peel, and core the pears. Place in microwave-safe dish and cover with orange juice and water. Cover and cook in a microwave on high for 6 - 8 minutes or until pears are fork tender. (Check the pears after 6 minutes; the fresher the pears, the longer they'll take to cook.)

Spoon juice over pears, cover, and let stand 30 minutes or refrigerate overnight.

To serve:

On the curved side (opposite of the cut side), take a tiny slice off the bottom, so the pear half will be stable in the dessert bowl. Place each pear in a dessert bowl.

Add berries or colorful sliced fruit. Top with a colorful sauce, such as, Marionberry or mint sauce.

Poached Pears and Dried Fruit in an Earl Grey Tea Sauce

Serves 4, but doubles nicely
Four dessert bowls

Note: May be made 1 day ahead. You will need at least 2-3 hours to chill pears and sauce, or else use an ice bath.

Ingredients

- 2 cups water
- 2 Earl Grey tea bags, decaffeinated
- 1/2 cup sugar
- 2 large firm but ripe Bartlett or Anjou pears (about 12 ounces), peeled, halved lengthwise, cored
- 8 dried apricot halves or 4 fresh apricots halved
- 4 whole cloves
- 1/4 cup dried tart cherries

Directions

Bring 2 cups water to boil in medium saucepan. Add tea bags. Remove from heat. Cover and let steep 10 minutes. Discard tea bags. Add sugar to tea and stir over medium heat until dissolved.

Add pears, dried apricots, and cloves, if using fresh apricots add them when the cherries are added. Cover and simmer until pears are just tender, about 5 minutes. Add cherries (and fresh apricots) and simmer an additional minute.

Using a slotted spoon, transfer pears, apricots, and cherries to bowl. Boil syrup in saucepan until reduced to 3/4 of a cup, about 5 minutes. Pour syrup over fruit. Chill until cold, about 3 hours.

Note: If you wish to serve immediately, put the fruit in the refrigerator while reducing the sauce. After reducing the sauce, submerge the saucepan in a large of bowl of ice and water. Stir until the sauce is at room temperature.

Divide fruit and syrup among 4 bowls and serve. If desired garnish with mint leaves.

Roasted Spiced Almond Pears and Figs

8 servings
Preheat oven to 450°F
Use an ovenproof skillet

Ingredients

- 1/2 cup sliced (or coarsely ground) almonds
- 4 firm-ripe Bartlett pears, 1/2 pear per person
- 1/2 pound fresh figs (if dried, they should be as soft as possible); about 1.25 figs/person
- 1/2 cup sugar
- 1/2 stick (1/4 cup) unsalted or sweet butter or 1/4 cup Full Spectrum
- 1 vanilla bean or 2 teaspoons of vanilla extract
- 1 teaspoon cinnamon
- 1/4 teaspoon ground allspice
- 2 teaspoons almond extract

Directions

Evenly spread almonds in an ovenproof 10-inch heavy skillet, and toast until golden, about 5 minutes. Transfer to a bowl and set aside.

Halve the pears lengthwise and cut each half into 3 wedges, discarding cores. Quarter the figs lengthwise.

In a skillet, melt the sugar and butter over moderate heat, stirring occasionally, until sugar is melted completely; remove the skillet from heat.

With a knife, halve vanilla bean lengthwise and scrape seeds into butter mixture or add vanilla extract. With a wooden spoon, stir in vanilla pod, cinnamon, allspice, pears, and figs until coated.

Place skillet in the middle of the oven for 20 minutes; and roast the fruit until pears are just tender.

Remove vanilla pod and with spoon stir in almonds until coated well. Serve the roasted spiced fruit warm.

South Sea Bananas and Pineapple

Serves 12
Pre-heat oven to 350°F
Baking time 30 minutes
Use 9x13 inch oven baking dish

Ingredients

- 6 bananas, peeled; each cut in fours, lengthwise and halved
- 1 small ripe pineapple, peeled, cored, and cut in bite-size pieces
- 2 tablespoons of lemon or orange juice
- 1 mango, cut in bite-size slices (optional)
- 1 teaspoon cinnamon and/or ginger powder
- 1 tablespoon brown sugar (optional)
- 2 tablespoons unsalted or sweet butter, melted (optional)
- 1/2-3/4 cup shredded coconut, sweetened or fresh

Directions

Layer bananas in the baking dish. Layer the pineapple pieces on top of bananas. Evenly drizzle lemon or orange juice over the fruit.

Sprinkle cinnamon and/or ginger over the fruit.

Optional, cut the butter into small bits and scatter over fruit. Optional, evenly sprinkle the brown sugar over the fruit.

Evenly sprinkle the coconut over the fruit.

Bake in a 350°F oven for 30 minutes or until the coconut is lightly browned and bananas are soft. Serve warm.

Pastries

Truly, there is something special about pastries made from scratch and served immediately out of the oven. Nearly every Chanticleer breakfast includes a pastry of some kind. The exception might be when the main dish or first course has a significant amount of flour or bread and adding a pastry would make the entire menu too heavy in carbohydrates.

This chapter includes over 20 pastry recipes. Of course, many of these can be altered with different spices, nuts, or fruits to create more variations. For menu planning, my goal is to ensure that guests will not have the same pastry more than once during any visit. I also try to rotate the kinds of pastries (coffee cake one day, scones the next, then muffins, etc.). Unless guests are staying for an extended visit, they might not even get the same kind of pastry more than once during their stay.

Selecting which kind of pastry should be served also depends on what the main dish will be. As a general rule, the more sweet the main dish, the less sweet the pastry should be.

A word about the chemistry of baking or how to get fluffier, lighter results...yeast-free pastries use baking powder and baking soda as a leavening agent. These agents are fast acting once they come in contact with liquid. A baker wants the agents' chemical reactions to occur in heat – that is, in the oven. Therefore the trick is to add the liquid to the dry ingredients just before it goes into a pre-heated oven. Because of this, all recipe directions are specifically ordered so that liquids are added in the last or second to last step. The oven is pre-heated and pans are oiled or greased before mixing and measuring of any ingredients. Any strudel toppings, glazes, nuts and/or fruits are prepared first; then set aside ready for a quick application or addition.

Caraway Rosemary Cornmeal Biscuits

Yields: 12-16 scones
Preheat oven to 400°F
Baking time 12-15 minutes
Use an ungreased baking sheet
Use a food processor with an S-blade

<u>Menu Hint</u>: These biscuits are wonderful with a very sweet main dish or first course. They have lots of flavor, and will not compete with the sweetness of other dishes.

Ingredients

- 1 3/4 cups all-purpose flour
- 1/4 cup cornmeal
- 1-3 tablespoon(s) sugar
- 1 tablespoon baking powder
- 1/4 teaspoon baking soda
- 2 pinches cayenne pepper
- 1/3 cup chilled unsalted or sweet butter, cut into bits
- 1-2 teaspoon(s) caraway seeds
- 1-2 tablespoon(s) fresh rosemary coarsely chopped
- 1/3 cup low-fat buttermilk
- 1 egg

Directions

Mix first six dry ingredients in a food processor.

Add butter; and process until the mixture resembles coarse meal. Add caraway seeds and rosemary; and pulse the food processor a couple times to blend the seeds and herb.

Pour the buttermilk in a measuring cup; and whisk in the egg. Pour the liquid into the flour mixture. Pulse the processor just until the dough starts to form. On a lightly floured surface, knead the dough a few times. Evenly divide the dough into 2 balls. Pat each ball into a 1/2" thick round. Slice or cut each round into 6 or 8 wedges. Bake for 12-15 minutes or until the tops are lightly brown. Many of our guests enjoy these biscuits with butter and jelly.

Havarti Cheese Biscuits

Makes 10-12 biscuits
Preheat oven to 450°F
Baking time 12-15 minutes
Use an ungreased baking sheet
Use a food processor with an S-blade

<u>Menu Hint</u>:   Pair these biscuits with a sweet main dish and/or a sweet first course. Or serve these with a savory dish that calls for no cheese.

Ingredients

- 1 egg and 2 tablespoons milk
- 1 cup all-purpose flour
- 1/2 cup whole wheat flour
- 1/2 cup rye flour
- 1 tablespoon baking powder
- 1/8 teaspoon cayenne pepper
- Optional: 2 tablespoons sugar
- 1/2 stick of chilled unsalted or sweet butter, cut into bits
- 3-4 oz cubed havarti cheese
- 1/3 cup minced parsley
- 1/2 teaspoon cumin seeds
- 3/4 cup milk
- 1 teaspoon poppy seeds

Directions

For the egg wash: in a very small bowl, beat an egg with 2 tablespoons milk and set aside.

In a food processor, blend the flours, baking powder, cayenne pepper, and sugar. Add butter; and process until the mixture resembles coarse meal.

In a mixing bowl, combine flour/butter mixture, with cheese, parsley, and cumin seeds. Slowly stir in milk until the dough is moistened.

Turn out the dough onto a floured surface and knead until the dough just comes together.

Roll the dough out to 1/2" thickness. Brush the dough with the egg wash and sprinkle poppy seeds on top.

Note: If you roll out the dough in a square, then you can reduce handling it by cutting it into small squares; otherwise roll out to 1/2" thickness and use a cookie cutter.

Place biscuits on an ungreased pan and bake for 12-15 minutes, until golden brown.

Onion Rosemary Biscuits

Makes approximately 18 biscuits
Baking time 12-15 minutes
Preheat oven to 400°F
Use an ungreased baking sheet
Use a food processor with an S-blade

<u>Menu Hint</u>:   These biscuits are wonderful with sweet dishes.
Serve the biscuits with butter, but no jelly or jam.

Ingredients

- 1 tablespoon of olive oil or canola oil
- 1 cup of onions, minced
- 3 tablespoons of fresh rosemary, minced
- 3/4 teaspoon of ground pepper (black or white)
- 2 1/2 cups of all purpose flour
- 2 1/2 teaspoons of baking powder
- 1/2 teaspoon of baking soda
- 5 ounces of cold unsalted or sweet butter cut in bits
- 1 egg, beaten with buttermilk, totaling 2/3 cup

Directions

In a skillet, sauté onion and oil until the onions start to soften, then add rosemary and pepper, continue to sauté until onions are soft and translucent. Set onion mixture aside to cool.

In a food processor blend the flour, baking powder, and baking soda. Add the butter, process until the mixture resembles coarse meal. Add the egg and buttermilk mixture, and then pulse the fod processor a few times.

Add onions and rosemary; pulse the food processor just until the dough comes together.

Turn the dough out on a floured surface, knead it a couple of times. Add more flour if dough is sticky.

Roll to 1/2-inch thickness. Cut into rounds; and place the rounds 2 inches apart on a baking sheet.

Bake for 12-15 minutes or until the tops are golden brown.

Savory Almond Biscuits

Makes approximately 12 biscuits
Preheat oven to 450°F
Baking time 12-15 minutes
Use an ungreased baking sheet

<u>Menu Hint</u>:   Pair these biscuits with either a sweet or savory main dish. I like serving these with the Apple Cheese Flan and any of the cheesy savory egg dishes.

Ingredients

- 1 tablespoon unsalted or sweet butter or canola oil
- 1 small onion, finely chopped
- 2 cloves of garlic, minced
- 1/2 cup almonds, toasted and coarsely chopped
- 2 cups all-purpose flour
- 1 tablespoon baking powder
- 1/2 tsp baking soda
- 1/3 cup chilled unsalted or sweet butter, cut into bits
- 1/2 cup low fat buttermilk
- 2 tablespoons parsley, fresh chopped
- 2 tablespoons herbs, fresh (e.g., sage, rosemary, and thyme)

Directions

In a skillet, sauté onion and garlic with 1 tablespoon butter or oil for 5 minutes; set aside and allow to cool.

In medium bowl, mix the flour, baking powder, and baking soda. Cut in the 1/3 cup of butter (leave it in small bits).

Stir in onions, garlic, buttermilk, almonds, and herbs.

On a lightly floured surface: turn out dough and knead until the dough just comes together.

Roll or pat the dough to 1/2" thickness. Cut dough with a biscuit cutter and place the rounds on baking sheet approximately 1 inch apart.

Bake for 12-15 minutes or until golden.

Apple Cinnamon Kuchen

Serves 12-16
Preheat oven to 350°F
Baking time: 1 hour and 15-30 minutes
Use a greased (with Pam cooking spray) and floured angel food cake pan.
Use a hand-held mixer

<u>Menu Hint</u>:   This makes an abundant, very dense and rich torte. Pairs well with savory egg dishes; may also be served as a dessert with rich dark coffee.

Ingredients

- 2-3 medium apples, peeled, cored and sliced
- 2 1/2 teaspoons cinnamon mixed with 1/4 heaping cup sugar
- 2 1/2 cups all-purpose flour
- 1 cup ground hazelnuts, pecans, or walnuts
- 1 tablespoon baking powder
- 1 cup vegetable oil
- 2 cups sugar
- 5 eggs, beaten
- 1/4 cup orange juice
- 2 1/2 teaspoons vanilla extract

Directions

Peel, core, and slice the apples; set aside. Prepare cinnamon-sugar mixture; set aside.

In a large bowl, whisk flour, ground nuts, and baking powder; and set aside.

In a medium bowl, blend oil and sugar, then beat in eggs, orange juice, and vanilla extract. Add this mixture to flour mixture. Using a hand mixer, blend the batter just until smooth.

Pour half the batter into the angel food cake pan. Evenly arrange half the apples on top and then evenly sprinkle half the cinnamon-sugar mixture on the apples. Pour the remaining batter into the pan and repeat the layering with the remaining apples and cinnamon-sugar mixture.

Bake for 1 hour and 15-30 minutes or until a toothpick inserted into the center comes out clean and dry.

Apricot Coffee Cake

Serves 6-8
Preheat oven to 425°F
Baking time: 40-45 minutes
Use an 8x8-inch baking dish greased with Pam cooking spray

Note: So yummy your guests won't realize that this recipe is low
in fat and high in fiber! Adapted from "The Healthy Heart"
cookbook by Adderly and Fulde.

Menu Hint: Serve with any savory egg dish and fresh fruit salad
for a first course. May also be served as a dessert with tea or
coffee.

Ingredients

Streusel:
- 2/3 cup flour
- 1/4 cup brown sugar
- 1 teaspoon cinnamon
- 1/2 chopped walnuts
- 1/4 cup corn oil (or vegetable oil)

Cake Batter:
- 1 1/2 cups sliced apricots
- 3/4 cup brown sugar, packed
- 1 teaspoon cinnamon
- 1/2 teaspoon cardamom
- 1/4 teaspoon allspice
- 1 cup all-purpose flour
- 1/2 cup whole wheat
- 1/2 cup oat bran
- 2 teaspoons baking powder
- 2 egg whites
- 1 1/4 cup light soy milk (or low-fat milk)
- 2 teaspoons vanilla
- 1 teaspoons almond extract

Directions

Streusel:

In a medium bowl, whisk flour, brown sugar and cinnamon. Add walnuts; then blend in oil. Mixture should be a little clumpy. Set bowl aside.

Cake Batter:

Arrange the apricots in one layer on the bottom of baking dish, sprinkle the apricots with 1/4 cup brown sugar and the spices, bake for 5 minutes at 425°F (alternatively: cook apricots, sugar and spices in a sauce pan, then pour in baking dish). Remove the apricot dish and reduce oven to 350°F.

In a medium bowl combine the flours, baking powder, and remaining brown sugar.

In a large bowl, whisk the egg whites until softly stiff; add the soy milk (or low-fat milk), vanilla, and almond extract.

Add flour mixture to liquid mixture, stir until blended, and then pour batter onto the apricots. Evenly sprinkle the streusel on top of the batter and bake for 40-45 minutes, or just until a toothpick, inserted into the center, comes out dry.

Blackberry Coffee Cake

Serves 8
Preheat oven to 350°F
Baking time: 40-45 minutes
Use 9-10 inch baking dish greased Pam cooking spray or butter

<u>Menu Hint</u>: Pairs well with any savory egg dish; may also be served at teatime.

Ingredients

Topping:
- 1/3 cup flour
- 1/3 cup sugar
- 1/2 teaspoon almond extract
- 1/4 cup unsalted or sweet butter, cut in pieces

Batter:
- 1/4 cup vegetable oil or shortening
- 1/2 cup sugar
- 1 egg
- 1 teaspoon vanilla extract
- 1 1/3 cup flour
- 1 1/2 teaspoon baking powder
- 1/3 cup milk
- 1 cup blackberries (may substitute blueberries) fresh or frozen (unthawed)

Directions

For the topping, in a medium bowl, mix the flour, sugar and almond extract and cut in butter until crumbly, set the bowl aside.

In a medium-large bowl, cream together oil or shortening and sugar until smooth. Add the egg and vanilla extract, and mix well.

In another bowl, whisk together flour and baking powder.

Add some of the flour mixture to the creamed mixture; then add some of the milk. Continue to alternate until batter is smooth (small lumps are fine).

Spread the batter into the baking dish and top with the blackberries.

Spread the topping over the berries.

Bake in 350°F oven for 40-45 minutes or until a toothpick, inserted in the center, comes out clean.

Buttermilk-Cinnamon Coffee Cake

Serves 12-15
Preheat oven to 350°F
Baking time: 40-45 minutes
Use a 9x13-inch baking dish greased with Pam cooking spray

Note: This recipe is based on and altered from Margaret S. Fox's coffee cake in the "Morning Food" cookbook.

Menu Hint: Quick to prepare! Serve with any savory egg dish; may also be served at teatime or as dessert.

Ingredients

- 2 1/4 cups all-purpose flour
- 2 teaspoons cinnamon
- 1/4-1/2 teaspoon powdered ginger
- 1 cup brown sugar
- 3/4 cup white sugar
- 3/4 cup vegetable oil
- 1 cup chopped walnuts or pecans
- 1 teaspoon baking soda
- 1 teaspoon baking powder
- 1 cup low-fat buttermilk (or low-fat milk + 1 tablespoon of plain yogurt, totaling 1 cup)
- 1 egg

Directions

In a large bowl mix the flour, cinnamon, ginger, both sugars, and oil.

Remove 3/4 cup of this mixture, and to it add the chopped nuts, and set aside - this makes the topping.

To the remaining dry mixture, add the baking soda and baking powder.

Measure out the buttermilk. Beat the egg into the buttermilk, and pour into the dry mixture. Mix the batter to combine all ingredients (small lumps in the batter are all right).

Pour mixture into the baking dish, and evenly sprinkle topping over the batter. Bake in 350°F oven for 40-45 minutes or until a toothpick, inserted in the center, comes out clean.

Custard Cornbread

Serves 6-8
Preheat oven to 350°F
Baking time: 60 minutes
Use a well-buttered 8"x8" baking dish

Note: This recipe came from "The Breakfast Book" by Marion
        Cunningham. I've made a few changes by substituting
        the cream for buttermilk, dispensing with the salt, and
        suggesting an "over-the-top" topping.

Menu Hint: Pairs well with any non-cheesy savory egg dish.

Ingredients

- 2 eggs
- 3 tablespoons unsalted or sweet butter, melted
- 3 tablespoons sugar
- 2 cups low-fat milk (optional: whole milk)
- 1 1/2 tablespoons white vinegar
- 1 cup all-purpose flour
- 3/4 cup yellow cornmeal
- 1 teaspoon baking powder
- 1/2 teaspoon baking soda
- 1 cup low-fat buttermilk or 1 cup heavy cream
- Optional: top with a lemon or orange sauce. For the recipes,
  please see the Sauce section.

Directions

Put the buttered baking dish in the oven to get hot while you mix
up the cornbread.

In a medium-large mixing bowl, beat eggs and melted butter.
Add sugar, milk, and vinegar; and beat well until all is blended,
set aside.

In medium mixing bowl, whisk together flour, cornmeal, baking
powder, and baking soda, and add to the egg mixture. Blend just
until the batter is smooth and no lumps appear.

Pour the batter into the heated dish, and then pour the low-fat buttermilk (or cream) into the center of the batter - do NOT stir! Bake for 60 minutes or until lightly browned. Serve warm.

Optional: drizzle a lemon or orange sauce over each serving.

Figs and Sage Cornbread

Serves 12-15
Preheat oven to 400°F
Baking time: 25-35 minutes
Use greased (with Pam cooking spray) and floured 9x13 inch baking dish

Menu Hint: This cornbread is appealing with both sweet and savory dishes.

Ingredients

- 1/2 cup vegetable oil
- 3/4 cup sugar or Splenda
- 2 eggs, beaten
- 1-3/4 cups all-purpose flour
- 1 tablespoon baking powder
- 1-1/2 cups yellow cornmeal
- 1 cup low-fat or non-fat milk
- 4-6 large fresh figs, chopped coarsely (optional: 6 fresh apricots or 4 fresh peaches or nectarines) tossed with 2 tablespoons of cornstarch
- 2 tablespoons sage, fresh and minced (optional: substitute rosemary or mix the two herbs)

Directions

In a medium-large bowl, blend the oil and sugar, beat in eggs, add sage and set aside.

In another bowl, whisk the flour, baking powder, and cornmeal.

Add flour mixture to oil-sugar mixture, alternately with milk. Stir in figs. Pour the batter into the pan, and bake for 25-35 minutes or until golden brown.

Apple and Walnut Muffins

Makes 12 muffins
Preheat oven to 375°F
Baking time: 15-20 minutes
Use muffin tins greased with Pam cooking spray

Note: This recipe is dairy-free; the apples provide all the moisture needed. The recipe comes from cuisinedumonde.com.

Ingredients

- 1-3/4 all-purpose flour
- 3/4 teaspoon baking soda
- 1/2 teaspoon cinnamon
- 3/4 cup sugar
- 2 eggs
- 1/2 cup vegetable oil
- 1 teaspoon vanilla extract
- 3/4 cup walnuts, chopped
- 1-1/2 cups grated apples (tart apples such as Granny Smith or Pippins)

Directions

In a medium bowl, whisk together the flour, baking soda, and cinnamon. Stir in sugar.

In another bowl, beat the eggs, vegetable oil and vanilla extract.

Pour the liquid into the middle of the dry mixture and add the walnuts and apples.

Fold until the dry ingredients are just moistened - don't over-stir!

Fill muffin cups 2/3 full. Bake in 375F oven for 15-20 minutes or until a toothpick comes out clean.

Basic Gluten-Free Muffins

Makes 22 muffins
Preheat oven to 350°F
Baking time: 12-13 minutes
Use muffin tins greased with Pam cooking spray

Ingredients

Spices, fruit, and nuts need to be added to the basic muffin. The combinations make for a wide variety of muffins.

The basic muffin:
- 1 cup rice flour (brown or white rice flour)
- 1 cup soy flour
- 1 cup sugar
- 4 teaspoons baking soda or 4 teaspoons baking powder
- 4 eggs
- 1 cup low-fat buttermilk, or soy milk with 1 tablespoon of soy yogurt
- 1/2 cup vegetable oil

Suggested ingredients:
Spice: nutmeg, cardamom, ginger, or allspice
Fruit/berries: 1/2 - 3/4 cup of currants, raisins, dates, or shredded coconut. With berries, such as blueberries, strawberries, or blackberries, coat the berries in cornstarch (2 tablespoons) to compensate for the additional moisture

Nuts: About 1/2-3/4 cups chopped: pecans, or walnuts

Directions

In a medium bowl, whisk together all the dry ingredients (including spice(s)). In another bowl beat the liquid ingredients.

Add the wet mixture to dry mixture, stir until just barely mixed, and then add whatever nuts, fruits, or berries you have chosen. Fill muffin cups 1/3 full - and I mean only 1/3 full.

Bake in 350°F oven for 12-13 minutes or until golden and a toothpick comes out clean.

Blueberry Spice Muffins

Makes 12 muffins
Preheat oven to 350°F
Baking time: 15-20 minutes
Use muffin tins greased with Pam cooking spray

Ingredients

- 1 3/4 cup all-purpose flour
- 1/2 cup sugar (see note below for sugar-free muffins)
- 2 teaspoons baking powder
- 1 teaspoon cinnamon
- 1/2 teaspoon nutmeg, freshly ground
- Optional: 1/4 teaspoon allspice
- 3/4 cup milk (low-fat or skim) or soy milk
- 1/4 cup vegetable oil
- 1 egg, lightly beaten or 2 egg whites well beaten
- 1 cup blueberries

Directions

In a medium-large bowl, whisk together the flour, sugar, baking powder and cinnamon, and nutmeg (optional, allspice). In a 2-cup measuring cup, pour the milk to the 3/4-cup level, and then pour in the oil so that total liquid is 1 cup. Whisk in the egg and pour the liquid mixture into the bowl and stir.

Fold in blueberries until they are dispersed throughout the batter - don't over-stir.

Fill muffin cups 2/3 full. Bake in 350°F oven for 15-20 minutes or until a toothpick comes out clean.

Note: For a sugar-free version, use Splenda instead of sugar, and increase the baking powder from 2 teaspoons to 1 tablespoon

Carrot Cake Muffins

Makes 12 muffins
Preheat oven to 375°F
Baking time: 15-20 minutes
Use muffin tins greased with Pam cooking spray

Note: This recipe is dairy-free. The pineapple, and to a certain
degree the apples, provide all the moisture needed.

Ingredients

- 1-3/4 all-purpose flour
- 1/3 cup packed brown sugar
- 1 teaspoon baking soda
- 1/2 teaspoon baking powder
- 1 1/2 teaspoon cinnamon
- Dash of mace
- 1 egg, beaten
- 2/3 cup pineapple, crushed in juice
- 1/2 cup vegetable oil
- 2 teaspoon vanilla extract
- 2 cups carrots, shredded
- 1/2 cup raisins, softened
- 1/2 cups apples, peeled and diced (tart or sweet variety)

Directions

In a medium bowl whisk together the first 7 dry ingredients.

In another bowl, mix together the egg, pineapple, oil, and vanilla.

Pour the liquid into the middle of the dry mixture. Add the carrots,
raisins, and apples.

Fold until the dry ingredients are just moistened - don't over-stir!

Fill muffin cups 2/3 full. Bake in 375F oven for 15-20 minutes or
until a toothpick comes out clean.

"Pecan Pie" Muffins

Makes 12 muffins
Preheat oven to 375°F
Baking time: 13-15 minutes
Use muffin tins greased with Pam cooking spray

Note: This recipe was adapted from "The Healthy Heart"
cookbook by Adderly and Fulde.

Ingredients

- 1 cup all-purpose flour
- 1 cup oat bran
- 1 tablespoon baking soda
- 1/2 cup + 2 tablespoons coarsely chopped pecans
- 2 egg whites
- 2 tablespoons vegetable oil (alternatively: pecan oil)
- 1/3 cup nonfat milk (or low-fat or regular milk)
- 3/4 cup maple syrup
- 2 teaspoons vanilla extract

Directions

In a medium bowl, whisk together the flour, oat bran, baking soda and 1/2 cup pecans.

In another bowl, whisk together the egg whites, oil, milk, maple syrup, and vanilla extract.

Pour the liquid into the middle of the dry mixture. Fold until the dry ingredients are just moistened - don't over-stir.

Fill muffin cups 2/3 full, sprinkle remaining pecans on top of batter.

Bake in 375F oven for 13-15 minutes or until a toothpick comes out clean.

Spicy Applesauce Walnut Muffins

Makes 12 muffins
Preheat oven to 375°F
Baking time: 15-20 minutes
Use muffin tins greased with Pam cooking spray

Note: This recipe is dairy-free.

Ingredients

- 1/2 - 3/4 cup walnuts, coarsely chopped
- 1-3/4 all-purpose flour
- 1/2 cup sugar
- 2 teaspoon baking powder
- 1/2 teaspoon cinnamon
- 1/4 teaspoon nutmeg
- 1/4 teaspoon allspice, freshly ground
- 1 heaping cup of applesauce
- 1/4 cup vegetable oil
- 1 egg, lightly beaten or 2 egg whites well beaten

Directions

Coarsely chop walnuts and set aside.

In a medium-large bowl, whisk together all the 7 dry ingredients.

In a measure cup pour the oil to the 1/4-cup level, then whisk in the egg. Blend the liquid, as well as the applesauce, into the flour mixture.

Fold in walnuts just until they are dispersed throughout the batter - don't over-stir.

Fill muffin cups 2/3 full. Bake in 375F oven for 15-20 minutes or until a toothpick comes out clean.

Zucchini-Chocolate Chip Muffins

Makes 24 muffins
Preheat oven to 325°F
Baking time: 15-20 minutes
Use muffin tins greased with Pam cooking spray

Ingredients

- 1/2 - 3/4 cup walnuts or pecans, coarsely chopped
- 2 eggs
- 1 1/4 cup sugar
- 2 teaspoons vanilla
- 1 3/4 cup zucchini, grated
- 1 3/4 cup all-purpose flour
- 1/4 cup whole wheat flour
- 1/4 teaspoon baking powder
- 1 teaspoon baking soda
- 2 teaspoons cinnamon
- 1/2 - 3/4 cup chocolate chips

Directions

Coarsely chop the nuts and set aside.

In a medium-large bowl, beat the eggs with the oil, sugar, and vanilla, and then blend in the zucchini.

Into a medium bowl whisk together the flours, baking powder, baking soda, and cinnamon.

Stir dry ingredients into wet ones; and add nuts and chocolate chip just until they are dispersed throughout the batter - don't over-stir.

Fill muffin cups 2/3 full. Bake in 325F oven for 15-20 minutes or until a toothpick comes out clean.

Apricot Pecan Scones (Laurie's Fancy)

Yields: 12-16 scones
Preheat oven to 400°F
Baking time 12-15 minutes
Use an ungreased baking sheet
Use a food processor with an S-blade

Laurie Myrick, who worked with us for the first couple of years, loved these scones. Whenever she was in the kitchen with me, she would invariably request scones with apricots and pecans, thus the alternative name for this recipe - Laurie's Fancy.

Ingredients

Topping:
- 4 tablespoons sugar
- 1 tablespoon low-fat buttermilk

Dough:
- 3/4 to 1 cup very coarsely cut dried apricots
- 2 cups all-purpose flour
- 2 tablespoons sugar
- 2 teaspoons baking powder
- 1/2-1 teaspoon nutmeg (generous)
- 1/4 cup (1/2 stick) chilled unsalted or sweet butter, cut into bits
- 2 eggs
- 1/3 cup low-fat buttermilk or whipping cream
- 1 cup pecans, whole

Directions

In small bowl, mix the topping ingredients and set aside.

Coarsely chop the dried apricots and set aside.

Mix the flour, sugar, baking powder, and nutmeg in a food processor.

Add butter and process until the mixture resembles coarse meal.

Add one egg, pulse the processor to blend; then add the second egg, pulse the processor just until blended.

Add the buttermilk, apricots, and pecans; pulse the processor just until the dough starts to form and pecans are coarsely cut.

On a well-floured surface, knead the dough two or three times. Evenly divide the dough into 2 balls. Pat each ball into a 1/2" thick round.

Buttermilk Raisin Scones

Yields: 12-16 scones
Preheat oven to 400°F
Baking time 12-15 minutes
Use an ungreased baking sheet
Use a food processor with an S-blade

Ingredients

- 2 cups all-purpose flour
- 1/3 cup sugar
- 1-1/2 teaspoons baking powder
- 1/2 teaspoon baking soda
- 6 tablespoons (3/4 stick) chilled cubed unsalted or sweet butter
- 1 large egg
- 1/2 cup low-fat buttermilk
- 1-1/2 teaspoons vanilla extract
- 2/3 cup raisins

Directions

Mix first four dry ingredients in a food processor.

Cut in butter until mixture resembles coarse meal.

In a liquid measuring cup, pour in the buttermilk, beat in the egg and the vanilla; pour the mixture into the food processor (you just saved yourself from washing an addition small bowl!).

Pulse the processor just until the dough starts to form; add raisins, then pulse a couple of times more.

On a well-floured surface, knead the dough a few times. Evenly divide the dough into 2 balls. Pat each ball into a 1/2" thick round; slice or cut each round into 6-8 wedges.

Bake 12-15 minutes or until tops are golden brown.

Cherry Almond Scones

Makes 8 or 12 scones
Preheat oven to 400°F
Baking time 11-12 minutes
Use an ungreased baking sheet
Use a food processor with an S-blade

Ingredients

Topping:
- 4 tablespoons sugar
- 1 tablespoon buttermilk
- 1 teaspoon almond extract

Dough:
- 2 cups all-purpose flour
- 1/4 cup ground almonds
- 2 tablespoons sugar
- 1 1/2 teaspoons baking powder
- 1/4 teaspoon baking soda
- 1/2 teaspoon nutmeg
- 1/2 cup chilled unsalted or sweet butter, cut in bits
- 1/2 cup low-fat buttermilk
- 2/3 cup Bing cherries pitted, frozen (unthawed) or fresh

Directions

Blend all topping ingredients and set aside.

In a food processor, mix all the dry ingredients. Add butter and blend until the mixture resembles coarse meal.

Add buttermilk and pulse the processor just until the dough forms.

Turn dough out on lightly floured surface; knead a few times, just enough to blend.

Evenly divide the dough in 4 balls. Pat two dough balls into 1/2-inch thick rounds. Sandwich half the cherries between the dough rounds pressing lightly to seal. Repeat with the other 2 dough balls and the remaining cherries.

With a pastry brush, liberally apply the topping over the dough and then lightly sprinkle sugar on top.

Cut each round into 4-6 wedges and bake on an ungreased baking sheet for 11-12 minutes.

Cinnamon Nut Scones

Serves 12-18
Preheat oven to 400°F
Baking time: 12-15 minutes
Use an ungreased baking sheet and a food processor with an S-blade

Ingredients

Topping:
- 1 tablespoon cream or low-fat buttermilk
- 4 tablespoons sugar and 1 tablespoon cinnamon

Dough:
- 3 cups all-purpose flour
- 6 tablespoons sugar
- 2-1/2 teaspoons baking powder
- 1/2 teaspoon baking soda
- 1 tablespoon cinnamon
- 3/4 cup cold unsalted or sweet butter, cut into bits
- 3/4 cup walnut halves
- 3/4-1 cup low-fat buttermilk

Directions

Combine the topping ingredients - cream, sugar, and cinnamon; and set aside.

Mix the first five dough dry ingredients in a food processor. Add butter, process until the mixture resembles coarse meal. Add walnuts and buttermilk, process until the dough just balls up.

On a well-floured surface, knead the dough (add more flour if dough remains sticky). Evenly divide the dough into 2 or 3 balls. Pat each ball into a 1/2" thick round.

Brush on topping and cut each round into 6-8 wedges.

Bake for 12-15 minutes or until the tops are lightly brown.

Crystallized-Ginger Spice Scones

Yields: 12-16 scones
Preheat oven to 375°F
Baking time 12-15 minutes
Use an ungreased baking sheet
Use a food processor with an S-blade

Ingredients

Topping:
- 4 tablespoons sugar
- 1 tablespoon low-fat buttermilk
- 1/4 teaspoon ginger, ground

Dough:
- 1 3/4 cups all-purpose flour
- 3 tablespoons sugar
- 1 teaspoon baking powder
- 1/4 teaspoon baking soda
- 1/2 teaspoon nutmeg
- 1/4 teaspoon ground cloves
- 1/4 cup chilled unsalted or sweet butter, cut into bits
- 3/4 cup low-fat buttermilk
- 2 tablespoons crystallized ginger, cut in medium pieces

Directions

Topping: In a small bowl, combine buttermilk, sugar and ginger; and set aside.

Mix first six dough dry ingredients in a food processor. Add butter and process until the mixture resembles coarse meal.

Add buttermilk and crystallized ginger until the dough just forms. On a lightly floured surface, knead the dough about 2-3 times. Evenly divide the dough into 2 balls. Pat each ball into a 1/2" thick round. Brush topping on top of scones, then sprinkle more sugar on top. Slice or cut each round into 6-8 wedges.

Bake for 12-15 minutes or until the tops are lightly brown.

Orange-Ginger Scones

Yields: 12-16 scones
Preheat oven to 400°F
Baking time 12-15 minutes
Use an ungreased baking sheet
Use a food processor with an S-blade

Ingredients

Topping:
- 4 tablespoons sugar
- 1 tablespoon low-fat buttermilk

Dough:
- 2 cups all-purpose flour
- 2 tablespoons sugar
- 2 teaspoons baking powder
- 1 teaspoon ginger ground
- 1/2 teaspoon allspice (optional)
- 1/4 cup (1/2 stick) chilled unsalted or sweet butter, cut into bits
- 2 eggs
- 1/3 cup low-fat buttermilk or whipping cream
- 1 to 2 tablespoons orange zest (grated orange peels without white pith)

Directions

In small bowl, mix the topping ingredients and set aside.

Mix first five dry dough ingredients in a food processor. Add butter process until the mixture resembles coarse meal.

Add one egg, pulse the processor. Add the second egg, pulse the processor again. Add buttermilk and orange zest, pulse the processor just until the dough starts to form.

On a lightly floured surface, knead the dough a few times. Evenly divide the dough into 2 balls. Pat each ball into a 1/2" thick round.

Brush on topping. If a crispy glaze is desired, then sprinkle additionally sugar. Slice or cut each round into 6-8 wedges.

Bake for 12-15 minutes or until the tops are lightly brown.

The Chanticleer Inn Chocolate-Chocolate Chip Cookies

Makes about 3-4 dozen
Preheat oven to 350°F
Ungreased cookie sheet

We serve these cookies on our buffet in the living room along with port and sherry. Chocolate lovers find these cookies irresistible.

My nevy Ari Hollander gifted me a 9-lb jar of Dilettante Chocolates' Ephemere Sauce in the spring of 2006. What to do with a huge jar of precious gourmet chocolate sauce? The answer had to be to swirl into the cookie dough. Thanks to Ari the recent addition of chocolate sauce and cocoa has elevated this recipe from just yummy to divine.

Ingredients

- 1 cup unsalted or sweet butter, softened
- 1 cup packed brown sugar
- 1/2 cup sugar
- 2 eggs
- 1/4 cup high-quality semisweet chocolate sauce
- 1 teaspoon vanilla
- 2 cups all-purpose flour
- 2 tablespoons baking powder
- 1/4 cup dark cocoa powder
- 2 cups quick oats
- 2 cups chocolate chips

Directions

In a large bowl, cream butter and both sugars until very light and fluffy; then beat in eggs and vanilla. Blend in chocolate sauce.

In a medium sized mixing bowl, whisk flour and baking powder. Sift in cocoa powder. Add to the butter-sugar mixture and blend thoroughly.

Stir in oats and chocolate chips, and mix well. Drop by tablespoons onto ungreased cookie sheet.

If dough is frozen bake for 14-15 minutes, if unfrozen bake for 12-14 minutes (time varies with different ovens).

Savory
Egg Dishes

Eggs, the incredible edible as the saying goes, are a breakfast mainstay; and provide a perfect basis for all sorts of savory dishes. As all of these recipes include vegetables and occasionally meat, one may also serve them for lunch or a light dinner.

This chapter is where you may find recipes that are high in protein and low in carbohydrate. Increasing the egg whites, or reducing/eliminating egg yolks and cheese, will create lower fat versions. For the first time in 2006, I planted zucchini and yellow squash in the herb garden. Thankfully the deer ignored the two young plants, and the crop was incredibly bountiful! A family may grow tired of the endless supply of squashes throughout a summer. Fortunately at a B&B, the guest list changes every 3-4 days, so a steady supply of squash and zucchini is not at all tedious, but makes welcome additions to the egg dishes. Now that we have gated off the backyard from grazing deer, I have plans to expand the vegetable garden to include a number of tomato varieties!

For a lovely breakfast or brunch balanced between sweet and savory, pair these egg dishes with any pastry and first course recipe.

Rustic Russet Pie

Serves 12
Preheat oven to 350°F
Baking time 45 minutes
Use a 9x13-inch glass-baking dish greased with Pam cooking spray

Ingredients

- 12-14 eggs (or 6 eggs and 10 egg whites)
- 2-3 tablespoons fresh basil and rosemary, minced
- Fresh ground pepper to taste
- 1 medium onion, diced or finely sliced
- 1 tablespoon of vegetable oil
- 1-1/2 cups broccoli florets, bite-sized pieces
- 1 cup snap peas, bite-sized pieces
- 1 pound red potatoes, sweet potatoes, yams and/or russet potatoes, coarsely grated and peeled (don't peel if using red potatoes)
- 1-1/2 cups grated sharp Cheddar (or 3/4 cup Cheddar and 3/4 cup Romano or parmesan)

Directions

In a large bowl, whisk eggs with herbs and pepper; set aside.

Sauté the onion in a large skillet over low-medium heat until onion is just translucent. Add broccoli and snap peas to the skillet and sauté until warmed through; add to the egg/herb mixture.

In a food processor, grate the cheese; add to the egg/herb mixture. In a food processor, grate the potatoes or yams; add to the egg/herb mixture.

Stir to evenly coat the vegetables, cheese and potatoes with the egg mixture. Pour contents of the bowl into the prepared baking dish, spreading the mixture evenly.

Bake until center is set, about 45 minutes. Cut into squares and serve warm.

Sausage-Vegetable Frittata

Serves 6
Preheat oven to 350°F
Baking time 30-45 minutes
Use a 9-inch glass baking pie pan greased with Pam cooking spray

Ingredients

- 6 eggs (or 3 eggs and 5 egg whites)
- 2 tablespoons fresh herbs, minced, select 2 of the following: basil, rosemary, oregano, sage, or thyme
- Fresh ground pepper to taste
- 1 medium-small onion, finely sliced
- 1/2 small red or orange bell pepper, diced
- 1 tablespoon of vegetable oil and 1 tablespoon of butter (or 2 tablespoons of oil)
- 2 chicken sausage links casings removed, finely sliced
- 1 medium-small zucchini or yellow summer squash, sliced, enough to line the bottom of the pan
- 1-1/2 cups vegetables in bite-size pieces, (asparagus, broccoli florets, snap peas, green beans, edamame, etc.)
- Optional: 1/2-1 cup grated sharp Cheddar (or part Cheddar and part Romano or Parmesan)
- Tomatoes, sliced and seeded, enough to decoratively top the egg dish

Directions

In a large bowl, whisk eggs, herbs and pepper; set aside.

Sauté the onion and bell pepper in a skillet over low-medium heat until onion is just translucent, then stir into the egg mixture.

In the same skillet, sauté the sausage until lightly browned, then stir into the egg mixture.

Line the bottom of the greased baking pan with the squash slices. Pour the egg mixture into the prepared baking dish, spreading the mixture evenly.

Layer the remaining vegetables over the egg and squash. Top the egg mixture with tomatoes slices. Evenly sprinkle the grated cheese, press down to moisten the cheese.

Bake until center is set, about 30-45 minutes. Cut into six wedges and serve warm.

Savory Strata Casserole

Serves 12
Preheat oven to 350°F
Cooking time: 50 minutes
Use a 9x13-inch glass-baking dish greased with Pam cooking spray
(Can be prepared the night before. Cover and chill, however bake
it uncovered.)

Ingredients

- White bread cut into cubes enough to line generously the bottom
  of the baking dish. Select bread with heft and body, day or two
  old is best.
- 1 pound pre-cooked turkey or chicken sausage, cut in small
  pieces (omit for vegetarians)
- Two or three kinds of vegetables, coarsely chopped, such
  as, broccoli, tomato, sweet peas, zucchini, mushrooms, bell
  peppers, etc. Enough to form a single 9x13 layer
- 1 cup grated sharp Cheddar cheese or a mix of Cheddar/Romano
- 10 large eggs, or 5 eggs and 8 egg whites
- 2 cups low-fat milk
- 2-3 tablespoons fresh herbs, minced, such as, basil, rosemary,
  oregano, sage, or thyme
- Pepper to taste
- 2 teaspoons dry mustard
- 4-5 drops Tabasco sauce, if sausage is not spicy

Directions

Spread cubed bread evenly across the bottom of the prepared dish.
Layer with sausage, vegetables, and cheese.

In a large bowl, beat together eggs, milk and spice/herbs. Evenly
pour egg mixture over the cheese.

Bake uncovered until casserole is puffy and its center set, about 50
minutes. Cut into 12 squares and serve.

Sherried Eggs with Vegetables

Serves 6
Pre-heat oven 350°F
Use six 6-oz. ramekins - one for each person
Use a heavy cookie sheet

Ingredients

- Oil - Pam Cooking Spray

Use enough of the next three vegetables to layer the bottom of each ramekin:

- Edamame (soybeans), shelled
- Mushrooms, such as, shitake or button
- 1 medium tomato, seeded and diced
- 2-3 tablespoons chives, fresh and minced
- 6-8 eggs, or 3 eggs and 6 egg whites at room temperature
- Fresh herbs, finely chopped - 2-3 of the following: rosemary, thyme, oregano, sage, etc.
- Freshly ground pepper, to taste
- 1/4 cup cooking or cocktail sherry (instead of sherry, use 3-4 drops of Tabasco sauce)

Directions

Liberally spray Pam on the bottom and sides of each ramekin. Evenly divide edamame, sliced mushrooms, tomato and chives among the ramekins.

In a large bowl, whisk eggs with the herbs, pepper, and sherry (or Tabasco sauce). Evenly pour the egg mixture into each ramekin. Sprinkle the grated cheese over each ramekin.

Place ramekins on a cookie sheet; and bake in the oven for about 20-30 minutes, or until puffy and just cooked through.

Serve in ramekins or pop them out.

Shitake Salmon Mini-Frittata

Serves 6
Pre-heat oven to 350°F
Use six 6-oz. Ramekins - one for each person
Use a heavy cookie sheet with edges

Ingredients

- 6-8 eggs (or 3 eggs and 6 egg whites) at room temperature
- 2 tablespoons of 2 fresh herbs: rosemary, thyme, oregano, sage, basil, etc.
- 1/2 cup cooking sherry or dry cocktail sherry
- Freshly ground pepper to taste
- Oil - Pam Spray
- 1 1/2 tablespoons of vegetable oil
- 1/2 cup - 3/4 cup onion, diced
- 1/2 -3/4 cup shitake mushrooms, sliced, tough stems removed
- 2 cups of 2 kinds of vegetables, coarsely chopped (suggestions, asparagus, spinach, broccoli, and/or edamame)
- 6-8 oz salmon, fresh, cut in small bite-sized pieces

Directions

In a medium bowl, whisk eggs, herbs, sherry, and set aside.

Liberally spray Pam on the bottom and sides of each ramekin. Place the ramekins on a cookie sheet.

In a skillet, heat the vegetable oil over low heat, add onions and ground black pepper; cook over low heat until translucent. If vegetables are cold, add to skillet and sauté until warmed through. Stir in shitake mushrooms.

Evenly divide vegetables, onion and mushrooms among the ramekins and then pour the egg mixture into ramekins.

Bake in oven for about 20-25 minutes or until puffy and just cooked through. Serve in ramekins or pop them out.

Tortilla Española (Potato Omelet)

Serves 6
Use a 10-inch non-stick skillet

This recipe was adapted from Mark Winkler, the innkeeper at Gurley Street Lodge B&B, in Prescott, Arizona. Mark was a warm and charming host. We enjoyed staying at his B&B on our 2006 winter vacation tour.

Ingredients

- 6 large eggs, whisked
- 2 tablespoons olive oil (divided 1 Tbs + 1 Tbs)
- 1 large onion diced
- 1 large clove garlic, minced or pressed
- Pepper, to taste
- 2 tablespoons minced fresh rosemary
- 1 pound red-skinned potatoes, and cut into 1/4 inch thick

Directions

In a medium bowl, whisk 6 large eggs; set aside.

In large skillet heat 1 tablespoon of olive oil, reduce heat add onion and garlic, and cook until soft and golden. Put the onions in the egg bowl, and add pepper and rosemary.

Add 1 more tablespoon of olive oil to skillet. Reduce heat; add potatoes, cook until golden brown (10-12 minutes). Toss potatoes frequently. Remove potatoes with slotted spoon on paper towels to drain. Set aside the skillet.

Add the drained potatoes to the egg/onion mixture and toss to coat potatoes.

Return the skillet to high heat; and pour in the egg mixture. Immediately reduce heat. Cook the eggs until the bottom is golden and the eggs are two-thirds set. Shake pan to ensure omelet does not stick.

Flip omelet by sliding it onto an oiled plate and then return it back onto the skillet to cook the other side.

Cut into 6 wedges to serve, garnish with sprigs of fresh rosemary.

Vegetable Salsa Frittata

Serves 12
Preheat oven to 350°F
Baking time 45 minutes
Use a 9x13-inch glass-baking dish greased with Pam cooking spray

Ingredients

- 12-14 eggs (or 6 eggs and 10 egg whites)
- 3/4 cup salsa sauce
- 2-3 kinds of fresh herbs, 2-3 tablespoons, minced, such as, basil, rosemary, oregano, sage, or thyme
- Fresh ground pepper to taste
- 1 medium onion, diced or finely sliced
- 1 small red or orange bell pepper, diced
- 1 tablespoon of vegetable oil and 1 tablespoon of butter (or 2 tablespoons of oil)
- 1 medium-large zucchini or yellow summer squash, coarsely grated
- 1-1/2 cups vegetable cut in bite-size, (broccoli florets, snap peas, green beans, edamame, etc.)
- Tomatoes, sliced and seeded, enough to decoratively top the egg dish
- (Optional) 1/2-1 cup grated sharp Cheddar (or part Cheddar and part Romano or Parmesan)

Directions

In a large bowl, whisk eggs with salsa, herbs and pepper; set aside.

Sauté the onion and bell pepper in a large skillet over low-medium heat until onion is just translucent, then add to the egg mixture.

In a food processor, grate the squash and spread a thick layer on the bottom of the baking pan. Layer the remaining vegetable over the grated squash.

Pour the egg mixture into the prepared baking dish, spreading the mixture evenly.

Top the egg mixture with tomatoes slices. Evenly sprinkle the grated cheese, press down to moisten the cheese.

Bake until center is set, about 45 minutes. Cut into squares and serve warm.

Vegetable Sour Cream Frittata

Serves 6
Set the oven to broil
10-inch non-stick frying pan
Flexible spatula -- resistant to high heat

Ingredients

- 6 eggs (or 3 eggs and 5 egg whites)
- 1/2 cup light sour cream
- Fresh ground pepper, to taste
- 3-5 drops of Tabasco sauce, optional
- 1-3 tablespoons vegetable oil
- 1-2 tablespoons fresh herbs -- two or three of the following: rosemary, thyme, oregano, sage, chives, etc.
- 1 clove of garlic, fresh crushed, optional
- 2-3 kinds of vegetables (enough to fill frying pan 2/3rds full) -- such as, diced onions, soybeans, broccoli florets, asparagus tips, tomatoes, sliced or wedges, peppers diced, mushrooms sliced (any kind), spinach, artichoke hearts, etc.
- 1/4-1/2 cup one to two kinds of sharp cheese (such as, Cheddar and Parmesan)

Directions

In a bowl, whisk eggs, sour cream, salt, pepper, and Tabasco sauce, and set aside.

Heat oil in bottom of frying pan, until very warm, and well below point of smoking. Start with the vegetables that need the most amount of time to cook - for example, peppers and onions - sauté in the pan on medium heat add the herbs. Progressively add remaining vegetables according to their cooking time requirements until all are hot and equally al-dente.

Get the frying pan just to the temperature where the egg will sizzle when it hits the pan, but no hotter. Pour the egg mixture over the vegetables and reduce temperature a little. Move a spatula around the edge of pan, gently get spatula under and lift the cooked egg up, tip the pan to allow uncooked eggs to run under the cooked layer. Continue to lift around the edges of the pan and allow the uncooked eggs to go under the cooked eggs, until no more eggs will run.

Sprinkle top with cheese. Place the pan under the broiler until cheese is just melted.

Cut into 6 wedges and serve.

Yam-crusted Vegetable Frittata

Serves 6
Preheat oven to 350°F
10-inch non-stick skillet
9-inch glass pie pan liberally greased with Pam cooking spray

Ingredients

- 6-8 eggs
- 1/4 - 1/2 cup salsa
- 2 tablespoons fresh herbs, minced - any 2-3: rosemary, thyme, oregano, sage
- 1 medium-large yam or sweet potato, peeled, sliced 1/4 inch, enough to line bottom and sides of the pie plate
- Fresh ground pepper (to taste)
- 1 tablespoon vegetable oil
- 1 clove garlic, minced
- 1 medium-large onion
- 2-3 kinds of vegetables (enough to fill frying pan 2/3rd up the side) such as, soybeans, broccoli, asparagus tips, peppers diced, mushrooms, artichoke hearts, zucchini, summer squash, etc.
- 2-3 medium Roma tomatoes, sliced or wedged
- (Optional) 1/4-1/2 cup cheese (such as, Cheddar, Parmesan, or Romano)

Directions

In a bowl, whisk eggs, salsa, and herbs; set aside.

Line greased pie plate with yam slices slightly overlapping. Also place slices up the side of the dish, such that the top edge is scalloped. Pepper the potatoes; put in the oven while preparing vegetable mixture - until yams are beginning to soften.

Heat oil in skillet, until warm, and well below point of smoking. Sauté onions and garlic in the skillet on low heat until the onions are transparent.

Starting with the vegetables that need the most amount of time to cook - for example, broccoli or bell peppers - progressively add remaining vegetables according to their cooking time requirements until all are warm. Evenly spread onion and vegetable mixture over the yam slices.

Pour the egg mixture over the vegetables. Lay tomatoes on top in a decorative pattern and sprinkle the cheese (optional) on top of the tomatoes.

Bake dish in the oven for 45-55 minutes, until puffy and eggs are set. Cut into 6 wedges and serve warm.

Sweet Dishes

Every other day we serve a sweet main dish. As much as people profess to prefer savory dishes, it seems that whenever we serve a sweet dish, all plates return to the kitchen empty! I come to believe that sweet breakfasts remind my guests of holiday breakfasts of their childhood.

If you require food low in carbohydrate, recipes in this chapter are not for you or your guests – best to select a savory egg dish. However, if you require dishes low in cholesterol and fat: you are in luck! Many of these recipes can be made to be very low in saturated fat – without sacrificing taste.

With liberal use of fruit, many of these dishes are sweet enough without any processed sugar. Other dishes are free of processed sugar; and with Splenda, some of these recipes are just fine for diabetics.

Almond Pear Clafouti

Serves 6
Preheat oven to 350°F
Baking time 45-55 minutes
Use a 9-inch glass pie pan greased with Pam cooking spray

You might be familiar with the traditional French Clafouti dessert (pronounced claw-foo-tea), from which this recipe is derived. Clafouti has made its way over the Atlantic in recent years and is now served in many upscale restaurants. Most commonly, cherries are used with a splash of Kirsch; this was the version I learned many years ago. Traditionally the French use whatever fruit might be in season and in the pantry. At the Chanticleer, we most frequently use pears. The Rogue Valley is famous for its pears - and when in season, there's nothing more honey sweet and juicy. That being said, apples, plums, blackberries, nectarines, peaches and cherries also are served to very tasty effect.

Based on my staff's on-going devotion to this recipe, the decision to add almonds must have been a momentary lapse of genius. This recipe continues to be the staff's all-time favorite sweet main dish.

Ingredients

- 1 cup of low-fat milk or whole milk
- 3 eggs
- 1/2 cup sugar or Splenda
- 1 tsp vanilla extract
- 1 tsp almond extract
- 1/3 cup flour
- 3/4-1 cup almonds, whole
- 2-4 pears, core, peel, and evenly sliced lengthwise about 8-12 slices per pear. (Optional: if skin is soft and colorful, don't peel the pears)

Directions

In the order listed above, add all ingredients (except the pears) to a blender. Blend on high, scraping the blender's sides if needed, until almonds are well ground.

Prepare the pears and arrange on the bottom of the greased pan in a pinwheel fashion, with the base of the pear sections toward the outer edge.

Slowly pour the batter into the pie pan - the pears will float so nudge them about to keep their pinwheel formation.

Bake in the oven until set, puffy and golden about 45-50 minutes.

Serve with savory scones or biscuits, a starter that does not use pears, and a side of sausage or bacon. Alternatively, instead of a pastry and starter, serve with a large helping of berry crumble with a side of meat.

Apple-Berry Dutch Babies

Serves 6-8
Preheat oven to 465°F
Baking time 25 minutes
Use six 6-ounce ramekins
Use a baking sheet with edges

Ingredients

Batter:
- 4 eggs
- 2 cups low-fat milk
- 2 cups all-purpose flour
- 2 tablespoons sugar
- 1 tablespoon vanilla extract

Filling:
- 1 tablespoon unsalted or sweet butter
- 2 tablespoons brown sugar
- 6-8 Granny Smith apples, cored and cut in chunks, optional peeled
- Spice(s) such as, cinnamon, nutmeg, and/or cardamom
- Optional, orange or lemon zest, and/or almond extract
- Pint of berries, fresh (if frozen, thawed)

Directions

Batter: In a blender, mix all batter ingredients: scrape sides of blender container to make sure the batter is very well blended.

About 5 minutes before cooking the batter, with ramekins on a baking sheet put them in the oven until the ramekins are very hot.

Remove the baking sheet from the oven and spray each ramekin with Pam, and put the tray back in the oven for a few minutes to re-heat the ramekins.

For the second time, take out the ramekins and immediately pour batter into ramekins - 1/2-2/3 full - put the ramekins and tray back into the oven. Bake for 20-25 minutes or until puffy and golden.

Filling: Sauté apples in butter and brown sugar. Add spices, lower heat and gently simmer until apples are just soft. Add berries; gently stir until berries warmed through.

To serve, evenly distribute filling among the Dutch babies, generously sprinkle powdered sugar on top.

As this dish is heavy on the fruit, I frequently dispense with a fruit starter and serve this with savory biscuits, sausage and smoothies.

Apple-Cheese Flan

Serves 6
Preheat oven to 400°F
Use one 8- or 9-inch glass pie pan greased with Pam cooking spray
Use heavy baking sheet or a sheet of aluminum foil to catch drips

Ingredients

- 3 cooking apples (Granny Smith or Gala preferred) peeled, cored and thickly sliced
- 1/2 cup brown sugar, lightly packed
- 2 teaspoons cinnamon
- 1 cup low-fat milk (or whole milk)
- 3 eggs
- 8 ounces shredded cheese: either Cheddar-Romano or Cheddar-Parmesan

Directions

Liberally spray Pam on bottom and sides of the baking dish.

Layer the prepared apples in the baking dish. Sprinkle brown sugar and cinnamon over apples. Place cheese evenly on top.

Whisk eggs and milk until well blended; pour over the cheese. Make sure the cheese is wet - some of it can be submerged.

Place dish on a baking sheet or foil and bake in oven for 1 hour, until the apples are tender and egg mixture is puffy and set.

Allow the flan to sit for a few minutes before serving.

Select a starter that does not include apples. Turkey bacon and cornbread goes quite well with the Apple-Cheese Flan. Fortunately, both the cornbread and flan require a 400°F oven, so they can be baked together. If using two shelves, be sure to cook the flan under the cornbread.

Apple Pecan Bread Pudding

Serves 6-8
Preheat oven to 350°F
Baking time 45 minutes
Use an 8-inch square baking dish with cover or foil, greased with
Pam cooking spray

Ingredients

- 1 1/2 cups skim milk (alternatively, soy milk or low-fat milk)
- 1/2 cup maple syrup
- 1 teaspoon vanilla extract
- 2 egg whites
- 2 teaspoon cinnamon
- Wheat bread, cubed, 1-2 inch, enough to make 4 cups
- 2-3 medium apples, enough to make 2 cups when grated
- 2 tablespoon lemon juice
- 1/3 cup raisins
- 1/3 cup pecans or walnuts (optional)

Directions

In medium bowl blend together the milk, maple syrup, vanilla, cinnamon and egg whites, and set aside.

Cut wheat bread into 1-2 inch cube pieces, enough to make 4 cups, and set aside.

Core the apples. Using a food processor, grate the apples, and then squeeze some of the liquid out of the apples. In a small bowl, mix lemon juice with grated apples.

Evenly distribute one-third of the cubed bread on the bottom of a greased baking dish.Cover bread with half of the squeezed, grated apples, half of the raisins and nuts. Pour one cup of the milk mixture over these ingredients.

Evenly distribute one-third of the cubed bread on top of the apple-raisin-nut layer.

Cover the bread with the remaining apples, raisins, and nuts. Evenly distribute the remaining bread cubes on top.Pour in the rest of the liquid ingredients. Lightly push the bread down so that the milk mixture soaks evenly throughout all layers. Sprinkle with more cinnamon if desired.

Bake covered (either with foil or a lid) at 350°F for 45 minutes. If the egg mixture is not set after 45 minutes, uncover the dish and bake for a few more minutes. Let the bread pudding stand for 5 minutes at room temperature before serving.

Cheese Blintz Cake

Serves 6-8
Preheat oven to 350°F
Use an 8x8-inch baking dish greased with Pam cooking spray

Note: To serve up to 12, double the recipe and bake in a 9x13-
inch pan

This recipe has a very cheesecake-like taste. For less of a cheesy
blintz, substitute either the fig-walnut or date-walnut filling. These
two non-fat, low sugar variations get the "two-thumbs up" from
the staff.

Ingredients

Batter:
- 3 large eggs
- 3/4 cup sour cream (or 3/4 cup non-fat yogurt plus 3 tablespoons
flour, or 3/4 cup yogurt cream)
- 1/4 cup orange juice
- 1/2 cup all-purpose flour
- 1/4 cup (1/2 stick) unsalted or sweet butter softened
- 3 tablespoons sugar
- 1 teaspoon vanilla extract
- 1 teaspoon double-acting baking powder

Filling:
- 1 cup (8 ounces) low-fat small-curd cottage or ricotta cheese
- 4 ounces cream cheese, softened
- 1 large egg yolk
- 2 tablespoons sugar
- 1/2 teaspoon vanilla extract
- 1 teaspoon fresh lemon zest
- 1 teaspoon ground cinnamon

Topping Options:
- Marionberry-Orange sauce
- Fresh fruit: strawberries, raspberries, peaches, etc

Directions

Batter: In a blender or food processor blend together all the batter ingredients until smooth.

Filling: In a blender or food processor combine all the filling ingredients.

Pour half the batter into the prepared pan. Drop the filling by heaping tablespoonfuls evenly over the batter, then carefully top with the remaining batter -- layers will mix a bit. (The cake can be covered and refrigerated for up to 24 hours. Return to room temperature before baking.) Bake until puffed and golden, 45 to 50 minutes. Serve warm, top with a fruit sauce or fresh fruit.

Blueberry Cream Cheese French Toast

12 servings
Preheat oven 350°F
50-55 minutes
Use a 9x13 baking dish greased with Pam cooking spray

Ingredients

- 4-6 ounces of light cream cheese or Neufchatel cheese
- 3/4 loaf of blueberry nut bread
- 1/2 pint blueberries
- 6 eggs
- 4 cups low-fat milk (or whole milk)
- 1/3 cup sugar
- 1 tbs. vanilla extract
- Optional, for topping: sour cream, fruit sauce, and/or fresh berries

Directions

Spread the cream cheese on the bread slices.

Place the bread in the bottom of a greased baking dish, overlapping the bread like fallen dominoes.

Evenly sprinkle blueberries on the bread slices.

In a blender (or large bowl) combine eggs, milk, sugar, and vanilla. Pour the mixture evenly over bread. Ensure all the bread is moist and then cover with foil. At this point, you could refrigerate the French toast up to 24 hours.

Bake in a 350°F degree oven covered for 50 - 55 minutes, uncover dish for the last 10 minutes. Bread should be puffy and golden, and the egg mixture set.

Cut in 12-15 pieces and serve with your choice of toppings: dollop of sour cream or Marionberry-Orange sauce and/or with a side of berries.

Cocoa Waffles with Caramelized Walnuts and Bananas

Serves 4-6
Preheat oven to 200°F
Use a waffle iron and a heavy skillet (not a non-stick coated pan)
Use small sieve/tea strainer to sprinkle powdered sugar
Many regular Chanticleer visitors never get these waffles, as I only make them when we have a small number of guests to breakfast. Contrary to how the name may sound, the waffles don't taste like "Coco Puffs" – instead they are light and crispy, with a nice nutty flavor.

Ingredients

Topping:
- 2 tablespoons unsalted or sweet butter
- 1/3 cup sugar
- 1-1/2 cups walnuts or pecans, halves or coarsely chopped
- 2-3 bananas, thickly sliced

Waffles:
- 2 cups all-purpose flour
- 1/4 cup unsweetened cocoa powder
- 4 teaspoons baking powder
- 2 tablespoons sugar
- 1-1/2 cups low-fat milk, warmed slightly
- 2 eggs
- 1/3 cup vegetable oil
- 1/3 cup (2/3 stick) unsalted or sweet butter, melted
- Garnish: Powdered sugar and warm maple syrup

Directions

Topping: Heat butter in a large skillet. The butter should be hot, but not to the point of smoking. Stir in walnut or pecans to evenly coat the nuts. Stir in sugar. If needed, turn up heat. Keep nuts moving (!) just until the sugar starts to caramelize. Take skillet off heat, continue to stir, then add banana slices and gently toss to coat bananas. Place the skillet in a warm oven.

Waffles: In a medium-large bowl, whisk together all the dry ingredients.

In a large measuring cup, warm the milk in the microwave; then beat in the eggs. Add milk and eggs to the flour mixture; blend well. Immediately, add the vegetable oil and butter; briefly beat until blended.

Into a very hot waffle iron, pour heaping 1/3 cup of the batter for each waffle. Bake the waffles until they are golden and crisp.

Plate waffles, top with nut-banana mixture, sprinkle with powdered sugar; serve immediately.

Crème Caramel Baked French Toast

12-15 servings
Preheat oven to 350°F
Baking time 50-55 minutes
Use a 9x13 Pyrex glass-baking dish

Ingredients

- 1 cup brown sugar
- 1/4 cup unsalted or sweet butter
- 3/4 - 1 loaf of cinnamon raisin bread
- 6 eggs
- 4 cups low-fat milk (or whole milk)
- 1/3 cup sugar
- 1 tablespoon vanilla extract
- 1/2-3/4 cup of pecan halves
- Optional, for topping: Sour cream, fruit sauce, and/or fresh berries

Directions

In a small bowl, mix or cut the butter into the brown sugar. Spread the mixture over the bottom of the dish. Microwave the baking dish in increments of 1-2 minutes, until sugar and butter mixture is mostly melted and bubbly.

Place the bread in the bottom of the baking dish, overlapping the bread like fallen dominoes on top of the syrup.

In a blender (or large bowl) mix until well blended the eggs, milk, sugar and vanilla extract. Pour evenly over bread. Ensure all the bread is moist and then cover with foil. At this point, you could refrigerate the French toast up to 24 hours.

Bake in an oven at 350° degrees for 50 - 55 minutes, uncover baking dish for the last 10 minutes. The egg-bread mixture should be set, and puffy and golden. Cut in 12-15 pieces.

Optionally and decadently, serve with your choice of toppings: dollop of sour cream or Marionberry-orange sauce and/or with a side of berries.

Crêpes

6 servings
Pre-heat oven to 170°-200°F
Use an 8-9 inch non-stick frying pan or crêpe pan
Use a heat resistant rubber spatula

Note: For crêpe fillings, see the following recipes. Both the date and fig fillings are so rich and sweet, that we serve one per person, and pair it with a fruit-filled crêpe.

Ingredients

- 2 eggs
- 1-1/2 cups skim milk (optionally, 2% milk)
- 1/4 cup plus 1 teaspoon vegetable oil
- 1/2 cup whole wheat flour
- 1/2 cup all-purpose flour

Directions

In medium bowl, beat eggs until smooth. Add milk and oil; and whisk until well blended. Add both flours; and whisk until mixture resembles pancake batter. At this point, you can cover batter and store in the refrigerator overnight.

Heat 1 teaspoon of oil in nonstick or crêpe pan over medium heat. Pour a scant 1/4 cup batter into the pan; and immediately tilt and rotate the pan evenly coating bottom of pan with the batter. Cook until edges begin to dry, and the center top is firm to the touch. Loosen edges with a spatula and flip crêpe. Cook an additional 15 to 20 seconds.

If you are immediately serving the crêpes, stack the crêpes on an ovenproof plate and put in the oven while finishing the rest of the batter and making the filling.Crêpes may be made the night before; and put in an airtight container (or Ziploc bag) and stored in the refrigerator. When ready to serve, reheat in a microwave.

Crêpe Fillings

All the fillings are the newest creations in this recipe collection. With two fig trees, I'm always looking for more ways to use figs. At a time when I was eliminating processed sugar from my diet, I was especially looking for ways to satisfy my sweet tooth without cheating. The fig-walnut concoction was created late one night during a rare sugar-craving episode. The fig-walnut combination's immediate and unanimous success with all testers -friends and staff alike - later inspired the date-walnut combination. So please enjoy these rich heavy fillings that are completely free of processed sugar. It doesn't get better than this!

Both the date and fig fillings are so rich and sweet, that we serve one per person, and pair it with a fruit-ricotta filled crêpe.

Berry-Ricotta Crêpe Filling

Serves 6
Use a hand-held mixer

Ingredients

- 1/2 cup low-fat ricotta cheese
- 1/4-1/2 teaspoon almond extract
- Sugar or Splenda, to taste
- 1 pint berries of choice, strawberry, blueberry and/or blackberries
- 2-3 tablespoons orange juice
- Optional, powdered sugar sprinkled over crêpes
- Optional, maple syrup, heat and serve in a small pitcher

Directions

In a medium ovenproof bowl, blend ricotta cheese, almond extract, and sugar.

Put the cheese mixture in the oven to gently warm through, until ready to plate the crêpes.

Just before assembling the crêpes, in a sauté pan, gently heat berries and orange juice.

To assemble the crêpes, spread 1/6 of the cheese mixture in the middle of each crêpe, spoon 1/6 of the berries on the cheese, and then roll up the crêpe.

Plate the crêpes and sprinkle powdered sugar over the crêpes before serving.

Date-Walnut Crêpe Filling

Serves 6
Use a food processor with an S-blade

Ingredients

- 4-6 dried large dates, softened in enough water to cover dates (save the water)
- 2/3 cups walnut halves
- 1/3 cup low-fat ricotta cheese
- 1-2 teaspoons cinnamon
- Optional, maple syrup, heat and serve in a small pitcher

Directions

In a food processor, purée dates, walnuts, ricotta cheese; add cinnamon to taste. If needed, add water to make filling the consistency of toothpaste. Put date-walnut mixture in an ovenproof bowl, and put in the oven to gently warm through, until ready to plate the crêpes.

To assemble, spread 1/6 of the date-walnut mixture in the middle of each crêpe spoon and roll up the crêpe. Optionally, serve with maple syrup.

Fig-Walnut Filling

Serves 6
Use a food processor with an S-blade

Ingredients

- 6 fresh brown turkey figs (or 8-10 mission figs)
- 1/2 cup walnut halves
- 1-2 teaspoons cinnamon
- Optional, maple syrup, heat and serve in a small pitcher

Directions

In a food processor, purée figs and walnuts; and add cinnamon to taste. Put fig-walnut mixture in an ovenproof bowl, and put in the oven to gently warm through, until ready to plate the crêpes.

To assemble, spread 1/6 of the date-walnut mixture in the middle of each crêpe spoon and roll up the crêpe. Optionally, serve with maple syrup.

Vegan Pancakes and Waffles

Serves 4
Use a griddle or waffle iron lightly greased with Pam cooking spray

Ingredients

- 1 cup unbleached flour
- 1/4 cup cocoa
- 1 1/2 tablespoons sugar
- 1 tablespoon baking powder
- 1/2 teaspoon baking soda
- 1 1/4 cups soymilk
- 1 tablespoon vegetable oil

Directions

In a small bowl, whisk together flour, cocoa, sugar, baking powder, and baking soda; and set aside.

In a medium bowl, beat together soymilk and oil. Gradually add the flour mixture to the soymilk mixture, whisk until well blended.

Pour 1/4 cup of batter onto a griddle or waffle iron pan sprayed lightly with oil at medium high heat, cook until bubbles form, flip, and cook about 30 seconds more.

Sauces

Over the course of a season, our sauces vary depending on the whim of the cook, and what is in the pantry and the garden. Every morning, like our pastries, all of our sauces are made fresh and from scratch: almost always created minutes before serving. Most of the time, these sauces top fruit salads, sometimes they are drizzled over French toast, crepes, or cheese blintz.

For most of these sauce recipes, the ingredient amounts may be adjusted to prepare the required yield and suit the chef's taste.

Cream Cheese & Sweetened Ricotta

Yields 1 cup
Use a hand-mixer

Ingredients

- 1/2 cup or 4 oz non-fat ricotta
- 1/2 cup or 4 oz Neufchâtel cream cheese
- 2-4 tablespoons honey (sugar-free alternative, 2 tablespoons of Splenda)
- 1 teaspoon vanilla extract
- 1/2 teaspoon almond extract

Directions

In a medium bowl, with a hand-mixer blend the cheeses until smooth. Sweeten to taste with honey or Splenda; then add extracts.

Cream Cheese Sauce

Serves 6, can easily be doubled or halved
Use a hand-mixer

Ingredients

- 8 ounces, whole or low-fat, cream cheese or Neufchâtel cheese
- 1/2 - 1 teaspoon vanilla
- 1/2 - 1 teaspoon almond extract (optional)
- 1-2 tablespoons honey or maple syrup (enough to soften the cream cheese, but not make it runny)

Directions

In a medium bowl, with a hand-mixer blend the cream cheese and extract(s) until smooth. Sweeten to taste with honey or maple syrup.

Lemon or Orange

Yields 1 1/4 cups

Ingredients

- 1/3 cup sugar
- 1 tablespoon cornstarch
- 3/4 cup water
- 1/4 cup fresh lemon juice or 1/2 cup fresh orange juice
- 4 thin lemon slices or orange slices
- 1 tablespoon grated lemon peel or orange peel

Directions

In small saucepan, use a whisk or fork to blend the sugar and cornstarch. Add 3/4-cup water. Whisk over medium-high heat until mixture thickens and boils, about 2 minutes. Stir in lemon juice, lemon slices, and grated lemon peel. Then allow the sauce to cool to room temperature. Strain the sauce before using.

Maple-Orange

This sauce is perfect drizzled over fresh fruit
The amounts will depend on how many servings are needed

Ingredients

- 1/3-1/2 cup orange juice
- Maple syrup, sweeten to taste approximately 1-2 tablespoons
- A dash or two of cayenne pepper
Or
- 1/2 teaspoon allspice

Directions

In a small bowl or measuring cup, whisk together the orange juice, maple syrup and cayenne pepper or allspice.

Marionberry-Orange

Use a microwaveable dish, such as a 2-cup Pyrex measuring cup
There are a number of variations on this theme
The amounts will depend on how many servings are needed

Ingredients

- 1/3 - 1/2 cup Marionberry jam
- Orange juice (enough to make the jam saucy and soft)
- Optionally, add one of the following. Amounts are guidelines, they should be add according to amount of sauce and to taste:
- 1/2-1 teaspoon cinnamon
- 1/2-1 teaspoon almond extract
- Few pinches ground cardamom
- Ginger to taste (fresh, candied, or powder)
- 2-3 teaspoons zest of orange or lemon
- 1/2 teaspoon allspice

Directions

Blend jam and orange juice in microwaveable dish. Microwave on high for 30-45 seconds until jam is melted. Whisk in desired spice or zest. Can be prepared in advance. Cover and store in the refrigerator.

Mint

Use a food processor with an S-blade
Use a small sieve
Yields approximately 3/4 to 1 cup

Note: Best to prepare at least 30 minutes before serving: may
be prepared a day in advance and stored covered in the
refrigerator.

Menu Hint: This sauce is very refreshing and delicious on fresh
fruit.

Ingredients

- 1 cup packed mint leaves
- 1/3 cup sugar
- 1/2 to 3/4 cup orange juice

Directions

Process the mint and sugar until well and evenly blended. Put in a
small bowl and stir in orange juice. Cover the bowl and refrigerate
until well chilled.

Pour sauce through a small sieve, reserve the juice and toss the
pulp.

Sweet-Peppery Mint

Use a microwave-proof dish, such as a 2-cup Pyrex measuring cup The amounts will depend on how many servings are needed.

Ingredients

- 1/3 to 1/2 cup apricot jam
- 2 cups lightly pack mint leaves
- Orange juice, enough to make the jam saucy and soft
- 2 pinches of cayenne pepper
- Optional, honey or sugar, to taste

Directions

In a blender or food processor, combine jam, mint leaves, orange juice, and cayenne pepper. Add more orange juice, honey or sugar, or pepper, depending on desired level of sweetness or tartness

Pour sauce directly on fruit. For a more refined look, pour sauce through sieve and discard the mint leaves. Optionally, cover and store sauce in the refrigerator for a few hours to over night so that the flavors will infuse, then pour sauce through a sieve and discard leaves.

Yogurt-based Sauces

The following sauces all use non-fat yogurt as the primary ingredient. These sauces are drizzled over a fresh fruit or are used to accompany many of the First Courses recipes.

Almond Honey Yogurt

Yields approximately 3/4-1 cup
The amounts will depend on how many servings are needed

Ingredients

- 3/4-1 cup non-fat yogurt or soy yogurt
- 1-2 tablespoons honey, warmed to be runny
- 1 teaspoon almond extract

Directions

Briefly microwave the honey so it will be runny.

In a small bowl whisk the yogurt. Add the honey and almond extract, whisk until well blended.

Banana Yogurt Cream

Yields approximately 2 cups
This one is for banana lovers – rich, creamy and nearly non-fat
The amounts will depend on how many servings are needed

Note: Prepare the yogurt cream about 6-8 hours before use.

Ingredients

- 3 cups non-fat plain yogurt or soy yogurt
- 1 medium-large very ripe banana
- 1-2 teaspoon vanilla
- Optional, sugar or Splenda, to taste

Directions

Drain yogurt in a paper towel-lined sieve set into a bowl in refrigerator for about 6-8 hours. Before serving, transfer yogurt cream to a food processor; add the banana and vanilla and puree until smooth. Add sugar to taste.

Mint Yogurt

The amounts will depend on how many servings are needed
Use a small food processor with an S-blade
Use a small sieve
Yields approximately 3/4 to 1 cup

Note: Best to prepare at least 30 minutes before serving: may be prepared a day in advance and stored covered in the refrigerator.

Menu Hint: This sauce is very refreshing and delicious on fresh fruit.

Ingredients

- 1 cup packed mint leaves
- 1/3 cup sugar
- 1/4 cup orange juice
- 3/4 to 1 cup non-fat yogurt or soy yogurt

Directions

Process the mint and sugar until well and evenly blended. Put in a small bowl and stir in orange juice.

Pour sauce through a small sieve, reserve the juice and toss the pulp. Stir in yogurt; add more sugar if desired. Cover the bowl and refrigerate until well chilled.

Yogurt Cream

Yields approximately 1.5-2 cups

The texture and richness of yogurt cream belies that this delicious concoction is nonfat!

The amounts will depend on how many servings are needed

Note: Prepare the yogurt cream about 6-8 hours before use.

Ingredients

- 3 cups non-fat plain yogurt
- Sugar or Splenda, to taste
- Optionally further enhance with almond, vanilla or citrus extracts

Directions

Drain yogurt in a paper towel-lined sieve set into a bowl in refrigerator for about 6-8 hours. Before serving, transfer yogurt cream to a clean bowl and stir in sugar to sweeten, but not remove tartness.

Note: What to do with the whey? When a recipe calls for buttermilk and you have none … add about a tablespoon of whey for every cup of milk or half and half. The whey, or a tablespoon of yogurt, will create a good substitute for buttermilk.

Special Diet Index

Dairy-free

First Courses

- Figs with a Raspberry Coulis
- Figs in Red-Wine Syrup
- Fruit Crumble
- Mango-Berry Mousse
- Oranges in Cardamom Syrup
- Pear Boat
- Plums in Orange Sauce
- Poached Pears
- Poached Pears and Dried Fruit in an Earl Grey Tea Sauce
- South Sea Bananas and Pineapple

Pastries

- Apple Cinnamon Kuchen
- Apricot Coffee Cake
- Apple and Walnut Muffins
- Basic Gluten-free Muffins
- Blueberry Spice Muffins
- Carrot-Cake Muffins
- Spicy Applesauce Walnut Muffins

Savory Eggs

Omitting cheese makes these egg dishes dairy-free
- Rustic Russet Pie
- Sausage Vegetable Frittata
- Sherried Eggs with Vegetables
- Shitake Salmon Mini-Frittata
- Tortilla Española (Potato Omelet)
- Vegetable Salsa Frittata
- Yam-crusted Vegetable Frittata

Sweet Dishes

- Apple Pecan Bread Pudding
- Vegan Pancakes and Waffles

Sauces and Toppings

- Lemon or Orange
- Maple-Orange
- Marionberry-Orange
- Mint
- Sweet-Peppery Mint

Low in Saturated Fat

For non-fat, please see the "No Saturated Fat Section" below.

First Courses

- Figs in Red-Wine syrup
- Roasted spiced Almond Pears and Figs

Pastries

- Apple and Walnut Muffins
- Apricot Coffee Cake
- Basic Gluten-free Muffins
- Blueberry Spice Muffins
- Buttermilk-Cinnamon Coffee Cake
- Carrot-Cake Muffins
- Figs and Sage Cornbread
- "Pecan Pie" Muffins
- Spicy Applesauce Walnut Muffins
- Zucchini-Chocolate Chip Muffins

Savory Eggs

Omitting cheese and reducing egg yolks makes these dishes low in fat
- Rustic Russet Pie
- Sherried Eggs with Vegetables
- Shitake Salmon Mini-Frittata
- Tortilla Española (Potato Omelet)
- Vegetable Salsa Frittata
- Yam-crusted Vegetable Frittata

Sweet Dishes

- Almond Pear Clafouti
- Apple Pecan Bread Pudding
- Apple-Berry Dutch Babies
- Crêpes
- Berry-Ricotta Crêpe Filling
- Date-Walnut Crêpe Filling
- Fig-Walnut Crêpe Filling
- Vegan Pancakes and Waffles

Sauces and Toppings

- Almond Honey Yogurt
- Banana Yogurt Cream
- Cream Cheese & Sweetened Ricotta
- Cream Cheese Sauce
- Lemon or Orange
- Maple-Orange

- Marionberry-Orange
- Mint
- Mint Yogurt
- Sweet-Peppery Mint
- Yogurt Cream

No Saturated Fat

First Courses

- Figs with a Raspberry Coulis
- Figs in Red-Wine Syrup
- Fruit Crumble
- Mango-Berry Mousse
- Oranges in Cardamom Syrup
- Pear Boat
- Plums in Orange Sauce
- Poached Pears
- Poached Pears and Dried Fruit in an Earl Grey Tea Sauce
- South Sea Bananas and Pineapple

Pastries

- Apple Cinnamon Kuchen
- Apricot Coffee Cake
- Apple and Walnut Muffins
- Buttermilk-Cinnamon Coffee Cake
- Basic Gluten-free Muffins
- Blueberry Spice Muffins
- Carrot Cake Muffins
- Figs and Sage Cornbread
- "Pecan Pie" Muffins
- Spicy Applesauce Walnut Muffins

Savory Eggs

Omitting cheese and egg yolks makes these dishes non-fat
- Rustic Russet Pie
- Sherried Eggs with Vegetables
- Shitake Salmon Mini-Frittata
- Tortilla Española (Potato Omelet)
- Vegetable Salsa Frittata
- Yam-crusted Vegetable Frittata

Sweet Dishes

- Apple Pecan Bread Pudding
- Crêpes
- Fig-Walnut Filling

Sauces and Toppings

- Almond Honey Yogurt
- Banana Yogurt Cream
- Cream Cheese & Sweetened Ricotta

- Cream Cheese Sauce
- Lemon or Orange
- Maple-Orange
- Marionberry-Orange
- Mint
- Mint Yogurt

- Sweet-Peppery Mint
- Yogurt Cream

Gluten-free

First Courses

- Caramelized Fruit with Ricotta & Cream
- Figs with a Raspberry Coulis
- Figs in Red-Wine Syrup
- Honey-Cream Cheese Stuffed Peaches
- Mango Berry Mousse
- Oranges in Cardamom Syrup
- Pear Boat
- Plums in Orange Sauce
- Poached Pears
- Poached Pears and Dried Fruit in an Earl Grey Tea Sauce
- Roasted Spiced Almond Pears and Figs
- South Sea Bananas and Pineapple

Pastries

- Basic Gluten-free Muffins

Savory Eggs

- Rustic Russet Pie
- Sausage Vegetable Frittata
- Sherried Eggs with Vegetables
- Shitake Salmon Mini-Frittata
- Tortilla Española (Potato Omelet)
- Vegetable Salsa Frittata
- Vegetable Sour Cream Frittata
- Yam-crusted Vegetable Frittata

Sweet Dishes

- Apple-Cheese Flan

Sauces and Toppings

- Almond Honey Yogurt
- Banana Yogurt Cream
- Cream Cheese & Sweetened Ricotta
- Cream Cheese Sauce
- Lemon or Orange
- Maple-Orange
- Marionberry-Orange

- Mint
- Mint Yogurt
- Sweet-Peppery Mint
- Yogurt Cream

Sugar-free

First Courses

- Fruit Crumble
- Mango Berry Mousse
- Pear Boat
- Poached Pears
- South Sea Bananas and Pineapple

Pastries

- Havarti Cheese Biscuits
- Onion Rosemary Biscuits
- Savory Almond Biscuits
- Figs and Sage Cornbread
- "Pecan Pie" Muffins

Savory Eggs

- Rustic Russet Pie
- Sausage Vegetable Frittata
- Savory Strata Casserole
- Sherried Eggs with Vegetables
- Shitake Salmon Mini-Frittata
- Tortilla Española (Potato Omelet)
- Vegetable Salsa Frittata
- Vegetable Sour Cream Frittata
- Yam-crusted Vegetable Frittata

Sweet Dishes

- Crêpes
- Berry-Ricotta Crêpe Filling
- Date-Walnut Crêpe Filling
- Fig-Walnut Crêpe Filling

Sauces and Toppings

- Banana Yogurt Cream
- Cream Cheese & Sweetened Ricotta
- Yogurt Cream

Vegan

These recipes become vegan when substituting yogurt with soy yogurt.

First Courses

- Figs with a Raspberry Coulis
- Figs in Red-Wine Syrup
- Fruit Crumble

- Mango-Berry Mousse
- Oranges in Cardamom Syrup
- Pear Boat
- Plums in Orange Sauce
- Poached Pears
- Poached Pears and Dried Fruit in an Earl Grey Tea Sauce
- Roasted Spiced Almond Pears and Figs
- South Sea Bananas and Pineapple

Sweet Dishes

- Fig-Walnut Crêpe Filling
- Vegan Pancakes and Waffles

Sauces and Toppings

- Banana Yogurt [Soy] Cream
- Cream Cheese Sauce
- Lemon or Orange
- Maple-Orange
- Marionberry-Orange
- Mint
- Mint Yogurt
- Sweet-Peppery Mint
- Almond Honey [Soy] Yogurt
- Banana [Soy] Yogurt Cream
- Mint [Soy] Yogurt
- [Soy] Yogurt Cream

Subject Index

A

Almond
 cherry-almond scones, 67
 fruit crumble, 26
 pear clafouti, 93
 roasted spiced almond pear and figs, 37
 sauce, almond-honey yogurt, 123
 savory almond biscuits, 45
Apple
 apple and walnut muffins, 57
 apple pecan bread pudding, 98
 apple-berry dutch babies, 95
 apple cinnamon cake (kuchen), 46
 carrot cake muffins, 60
 cheese flan, 97
 fruit crumble, 26
 kuchen, apple cinnamon cake, 46
Applesauce, 62
Apricot
 apricot pecan scones, 64
 coffee cake, 48
 cornbread, 56
 carmelized fruit, 23
 dried, 35
 fruit crumble, 26
 poached pears and dried fruit and Earl
  Grey Tea sauce, 35
 Ashland, city of, 16

B

Banana
 mango-berry mousse, 29
 cocoa waffles with caramelized
  walnuts, 103
 south sea bananas and pineapple, 38
 yogurt cream, banana, 124
Berry
 apple-berry dutch babies, 95
 basic gluten-free muffins, 58
 berry-ricotta crêpe filling, 108
 blackberry coffee cake, 50
 blueberry cream cheese French toast, 102
 blueberry spice muffins, 59
 cheese blintz cake, 100

figs with a raspberry coulis, 24
 fruit crumble, 26
 mango berry mousse, 29
 marionberry-orange sauce, 119
Biscuits
 caraway rosemay cornmeal, 41
 Havarti cheese, 42
 onion rosemary, 44
 savory almond, 45
Blackberry
 coffee cake, 50
Blintz
 cheese cake, 100
 date-walnut filling, 109
 fig-walnut filling, 110
Blueberry
 french toast, cream cheese, 102
 muffins, 59
 crème caramel baked french toast, 105
Buttermilk
 cinnamon coffee cake, 52

C

Cake
 apple cinnamon kuchen, 46
 apricot coffee, 48
 blackberry coffee, 50
 buttermilk-cinnamon coffee, 52
Caraway Seeds, 41
Cardamom, oranges in cardamom syrup
Chanticleer Inn, 16
 breakfasts, 11
Cheese, aged
 apple cheese flan, 97
 Havarti, 42
 Stilton, 25
Cheese, soft
 berry-ricotta crêpe filling, 108
 blueberry cream cheese French toast, 102
 carmelized fruit, 23
 cheese blintz cake, 100
 honey-cream stuffed peaches, 28
 cream cheese sauce, 116
 cream cheese & sweetened ricotta
  sauce, 115